“*Enemy Alien* is a powerful and superbly illustrated examination of internment during World War One. nicole marie burton's haunting drawings skillfully complement the anonymous author, and Kassandra Luciuk's i provides important historical context. This bo addition to the growing field of graphic histor

—The Graphic History Collective

“In legend, the First World War marked the birth of Canada. In reality, it represented the apogee of one brutally militarized version of a particular vision of ‘Anglo Canada.’ Vividly told from the perspective of Ukrainians detained in concentration camps, and then sent as forced labourers to Cape Breton, *Enemy Alien* brilliantly reveals both how these men were victimized as ‘aliens’—and how they stubbornly resisted as flesh-and-blood human beings.”

—Ian McKay, historian and chair of the L.R. Wilson Institute for Canadian History, McMaster University

“All the more troubling for being a true account of the crippling legacy of Canada's first national internment operations, *Enemy Alien* obliges us to look at an injustice that left its victims afraid to speak of what they had endured, even as Ottawa's men tried to erase this history. An evocatively graphic refutation of their ploy and a unique portrayal of a wrong once almost deleted from our national conscience.”

—Borys Sydoruk, chair, Ukrainian Canadian Civil Liberties Foundation

“The illustrated world of *Enemy Alien* rings so true, in all its black, white and many greys. It's a gift to our understanding of Canada and of ourselves.”

—Melony Ward, publisher, Canada's National History Society

"This bleak moment in Canadian history should be part of our children's history lessons. Kassandra Luciuk has done a wonderful job bringing this historical event to life."

—INKY MARK, former Member of Parliament representing the Manitoba riding of Dauphin—Swan River—Marquette

"A vivid slice of Canadian history told in innovative comic-book style. *Enemy Alien* presents a powerful vindication of immigrants who, then and now, contribute to building a better Canada."

—SUZANNE BERLINER WEISS, author of *Holocaust to Resistance: My Journey*

"Haunting, infuriating, illuminating, inspiring, and gorgeously illustrated, this graphic history, based on a never-before-available memoir, tells the story of a young Ukrainian immigrant who, dubbed an enemy alien, experienced first-hand the brutality of incarceration during his internment by the Canadian state during the First World War. The mystery of the memoir's narrator—an unknown man and an everyman, disillusioned with the supposed pillars of western democracy—leads to a clarity of insight that will resonate with many readers and stimulate plenty of debate. At a time when the world is seething with intense anti-migrant racism, this is a timely, must-read history."

—FRANCA IACOVETTA, historian and author of *Gatekeepers: Reshaping Immigrant Lives in Cold War Canada*

"Expertly narrated and beautifully illustrated, *Enemy Alien* has much to teach us about the injustices of war, internment, and political repression, past and present."

—SEAN CARLETON, historian and assistant professor at Mount Royal University

Enemy Alien

a true story of life
behind barbed wire

written by
kassandra luciuk

illustrated by
nicole marie burton

Between the Lines
Toronto

First published in 2020 by
Between the Lines
401 Richmond Street West
Studio 281
Toronto, Ontario M5V 3A8
Canada
1-800-718-7201
www.btlbooks.com

Cataloguing in Publication information available from Library and Archives Canada
ISBN 9781771134729

Designed by DEEVE

Printed in Canada

MIX
Paper from responsible sources
FSC www.fsc.org FSC® C103567

GCC/IBT 1292 M

This project has been made possible by a grant from the Endowment Council of the Canadian First World War Internment Recognition Fund.

1914-1920

internmentcanada.ca

We acknowledge for their financial support of our publishing activities: the Government of Canada; the Canada Council for the Arts; and the Government of Ontario through the Ontario Arts Council, the Ontario Book Publishers Tax Credit program, and Ontario Creates.

Canada
Canada Council for the Arts
Conseil des Arts du Canada
ONTARIO CREATES
ONTARIO ARTS COUNCIL
CONSEIL DES ARTS DE L'ONTARIO
an Ontario government agency
un organisme du gouvernement de l'Ontario

To all who were interned behind Canadian barbed wire

Introduction

This graphic history began when I was researching the experiences of Ukrainian internees incarcerated in Canada during the First World War. The goal of my research was to both explore traditional understandings of internee identities and to rethink them more aptly as forced labourers, non-white migrants, political activists, and participants in an organized ethnic community.

I was also interested in examining the impact of the internment operations on the collective consciousness of Ukrainian Canadians. Did the internees simply reintegrate into their otherwise-untouched communities? Were they inclined to strip away any associations with Ukrainianness in favour of something more palatable to the Anglo-Canadian mainstream? Or did the internment operations radicalize their victims, triggering a mass migration into progressive outfits—like the Ukrainian Labour Farmer Temple Association (ULFTA)—which offered an explanation for their captivity by pointing to the interconnected nature of capitalism and Anglo-white supremacy?

Finding the answers to these questions required a creative approach to gathering sources. The personal side of internment is seldom found in the materials I habitually trusted as a historian. Instead, I would have to turn to the community and rely on the record keeping of organizations and activists who were operative at the time. I was admittedly concerned about what, if anything, I would find. But a chance encounter with the keeper of a private archival collection revealed a remarkable volume of previously unseen material that shed new light on the internee experience.

One document in particular stood out. It was the memoir of a man who was interned in Kapuskasing between 1914 and 1917. The tremendous significance of the source was immediately apparent. To this day, it remains the only comprehensive account of First World War internment written by an internee. While the recovery of such a document is noteworthy in itself, there is an added value in its ability to centre the voice of an insider within a history that has long relied on others to craft its narrative. Perhaps most notably, however, it presents the internment operations in a much larger context than was previously understood. Indeed, the author makes clear that this story neither begins nor ends with the internment operations.

By tracing the plight of a migrant lured to Canada with the promise of prosperity, only to encounter a much harsher reality on the ground, the memoir offers critical insight into the way in which internees understood their incarceration. Internment, while abhorrent, was not a lone enterprise or isolated event; it was part and parcel of Canada's longstanding and unjust treatment toward populations it deemed "undesirable others." In other words, the memoir effectively shows that internment was not a regretful anomaly, but rather part of the regular functioning of nation building. The bodies of undesirable migrants could be used to build the country, but they could not join it.

Ukrainians first began migrating to Canada en masse in 1891. Most arrived from the Austrian crownlands of Galicia and Bukovyna, two of the poorest and most overpopulated areas in all of Europe. Their migration was encouraged by the efforts of Clifford Sifton, Canada's Minister of the Interior, who was recruiting the foot soldiers of settler-colonialism on the Prairies.

Life for this so-called first wave of migrants was difficult. Those who managed to settle on homesteads struggled with outdated technology, limited capital, a challenging climate, poor land quality, and insufficient experience with large-scale agriculture. The majority, recruited into the labour-intensive industries of railroad building, mining, and lumbering, faced exploitation from their employers, who threatened deportation at even the slightest inkling of defiance.

As migration rates increased in the early twentieth century, many migrants found themselves held captive in immigration sheds, where they were auctioned off like cattle to private companies looking for cheap sources of labour. This was the case for the author of the memoir. Arriving in Canada in 1912, he could not afford to pay the $25 fee required to be released from the sheds. This peremptory and discriminatory policy was designed to funnel recent migrants into predatory work gangs, ever more cheap fuel to facilitate capitalist accumulation. Conditions only worsened when the majority of railroad construction was completed at the same time as agricultural mechanization took hold. This meant that for migrant workers, particularly those from southern and eastern Europe, there was little work in the years leading up to the First World War.

By the time the war broke out, then, the majority of Ukrainians were already familiar with the often-brutal reality of the migrant experience in Canada. It was perhaps no surprise to most when widespread xenophobia began to grip the public imagination and they became targets of outright hostility and calls for swift assimilation. Nor would they have been shocked when the government officially announced its decision to begin arresting those deemed "enemy aliens," which, in the case of the Ukrainians, was a result of their Austro-Hungarian passports.

The reasons for being picked up by the police were highly varied, running the gamut from trying to cross the border in search of work to simply looking suspicious, as was the case with the author of the memoir. Those arrested after 1917 were often interned for more political reasons, having been deemed "radical aliens" in response to rising worker militancy in Canada, Russia's October Revolution, and the ensuing first Red Scare. All in all, 8,579 people were interned between 1914 and 1920, the majority of whom were Ukrainian. An additional 80,000 others were forced to register and report regularly to local police.

The everyday experiences of internees oscillated from inescapable boredom to the indignity of forced labour. By and large, they responded with insubordination and resistance, including work slowdowns and eventually riots. In total, 107 internees died in the camps. Their deaths were caused by trying to escape, work-related injuries, infectious diseases, drowning, and suicide.

Beginning in 1916, the government began granting internees parole in order to fill wartime labour shortages in railway construction, mining, and agriculture. The internees, however, were averse to continuing their exploitation willingly and only left the camps by the force of a bayonet. The author of the memoir, for example, was released into the custody of the Dominion Steel and Coal Corporation (DOSCO) in Sydney, Nova Scotia. When armistice was declared, he was not free to go, only leaving Sydney in 1923 after he was blacklisted for joining a union and going on strike.

The memoir concludes with the author's return to Kapuskasing in 1945. By the time of his reunion with the town, the overall situation of Ukrainians in Canada had somewhat improved. But for the author, a member of the progressive left, the renewed political repression under Section 98 and the Defence of Canada Regulations (DOCR), both extensions of the draconian *War Measures Act*, was still fresh. Within a year, Canada's second Red Scare would take hold, further and disproportionately afflicting the "foreign born."

It is because of this expansive framing that the memoir serves as the perfect basis for a graphic history. For those previously unaware of the internment operations, it situates the event in a comprehensive way, wherein readers can draw parallels to historical events and experiences more familiar to them. For those with previous exposure, especially members of the Ukrainian Canadian community, the memoir challenges an ethnic particularism that conceptualizes the internment operations as a sui generis or unprecedented event and invites readers to make connections to the experiences of migrants, and the disciplinary regimes that oversee them, across the globe.

Just as the memoir provides new possibilities for understanding the internment operations, it also poses several weighty challenges. Most critically, the author remains unknown. The most probable theory is that it was penned by John Boychuk, an activist and organizer with the ULFTA. This is substantiated by several key pieces of evidence. First, someone by the name of John Boychuk was, in fact, interned in Kapuskasing. Second, there is a photograph of Boychuk in the Kapuskasing cemetery from 1945, which lines up with the author's timeline of returning to the town. Third, much like the author, Boychuk was active in the mining unions after being released and spent some time on the east coast working with the United Mine Workers of America.

Boychuk is an especially compelling subject because, in 1931, he was arrested alongside Tim Buck, the general secretary of the Communist Party of Canada (CPC), under the expansive powers of Section 98. Several years later, he was again incarcerated during the Second World War under the DOCR-mandated crackdown on communism. While being caught up in three of the twentieth century's most prominent instances of political policing would surely explain Boychuk's desire to write a memoir of this kind, several issues regarding his authorship emerged. As a prominent figure, Boychuk left a modest archival record and was the subject of tremendous police surveillance. His incarceration in this period is not mentioned in either his private holdings or in state records. An especially damning clue arises from his 1953 federal election campaign where he ran for the Labour-Progressive Party in Parkdale–High Park. In the press coverage of his campaign, his captivity in the 1930s and 1940s is covered in detail, but again, there is no mention of the First World War.

The most significant evidence against Boychuk's authorship is inconsistencies in the timeline both before and after the internment of the First World War. The author of the memoir writes that he arrived in Canada in 1912, but Boychuk arrived in 1913. Moreover, the author was interned in 1914 and paroled to DOSCO in 1917, remaining in Nova Scotia until at least 1923. Boychuk, on the other hand, was arrested in Toronto in 1918 for possession of seditious literature and served a year before being released on parole. He was arrested again for a similar offence in 1919 and served an additional 18 months. Given this evidence, it is all but impossible for Boychuk to have written the memoir.

Leaving one's name off of one's own memoir is telling of the ongoing fear of repression that was so clearly prominent in the author's life. That he was uncomfortable claiming this work as his own reinforces longstanding claims by scholars and activists that, even after their incarceration, Ukrainians long remained in fear of the barbed wire fence.

Anonymity, however justified, makes it impossible to piece together a comprehensive biography. It likewise adds an element of uncertainty to the narrative that is reproduced in the graphic novel. This is made more complicated by the fact that the memoir was written in 1945, some

30 years after the author's incarceration. Because of these complications, I have taken great care to ensure the accuracy of the memoir by identifying certain unforgeable claims and comparing the document to available evidence. Little has been done to editorialize the text beyond necessary additions for clarity and colour.

Despite the memoir likely not belonging to Boychuk, I have chosen to retain his name as the protagonist for several reasons. Several John Boychuks were interned during the First World War. Boychuk's experiences are also more similar than not to those of the average Ukrainian Canadian internee. While the particulars of Boychuk's political participation are less definitive, the undercurrents of his lived experiences are quite typical. Lastly, John Boychuk is roughly the equivalent of John Smith in English. This name, then, represents the quintessential everyman on whom the story of internment can be projected. Until further first-hand accounts are recovered, my hope is that all internees can be seen through Boychuk's eyes, whoever he may have been.

—*Kassandra Luciuk*

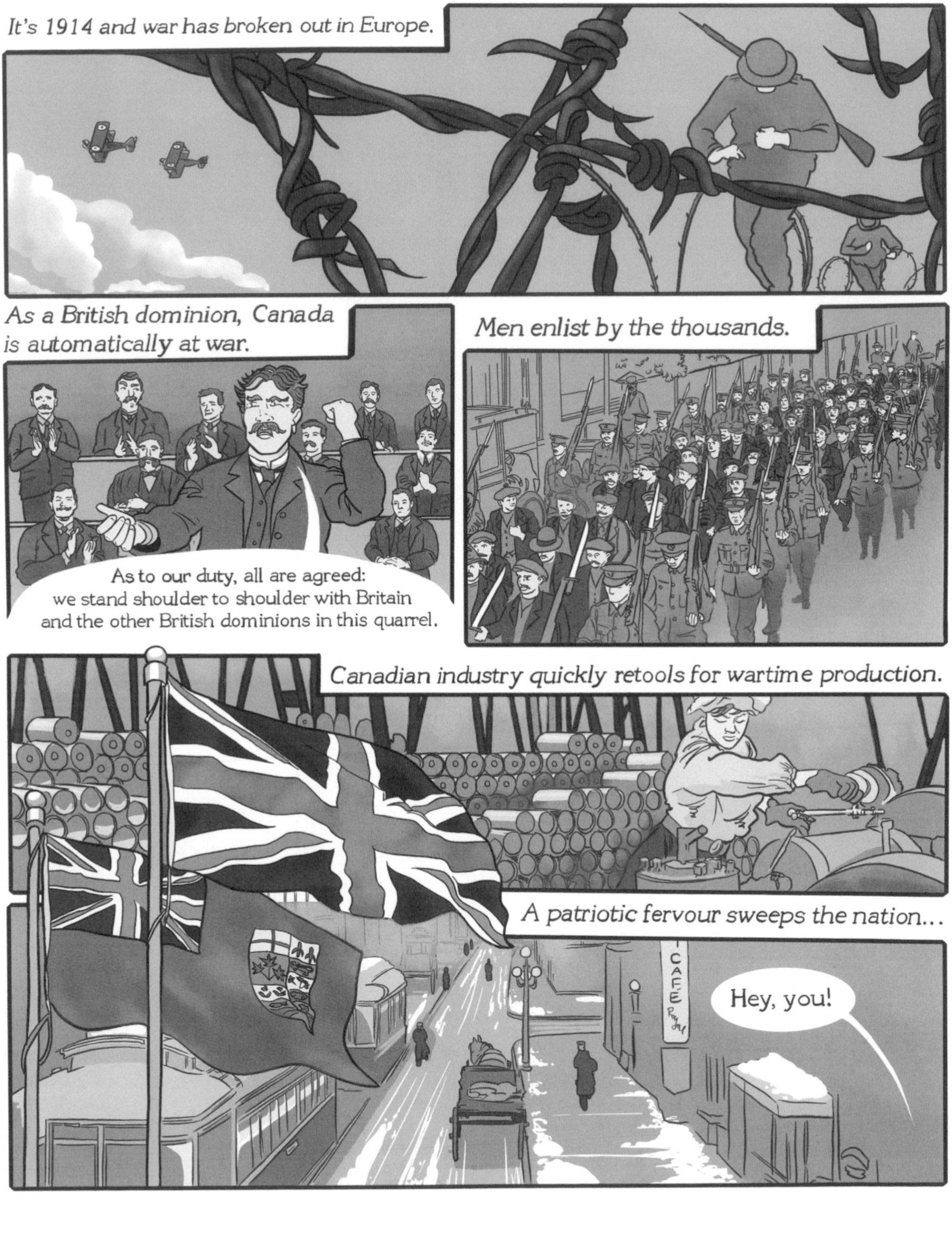
It's 1914 and war has broken out in Europe.
As a British dominion, Canada is automatically at war.
As to our duty, all are agreed: we stand shoulder to shoulder with Britain and the other British dominions in this quarrel.
Men enlist by the thousands.
Canadian industry quickly retools for wartime production.
A patriotic fervour sweeps the nation...
CAFE
Hey, you!

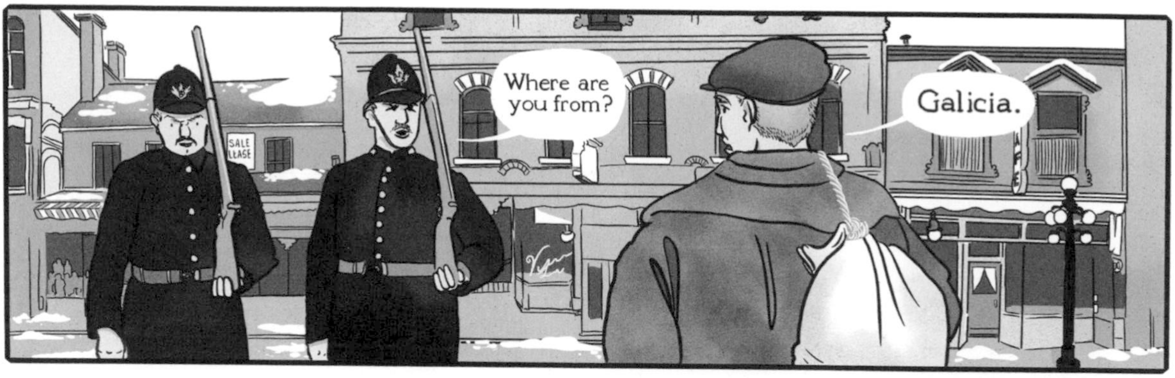
Where are you from?
Galicia.

...and in the streets of Toronto, a man is stopped by the police.

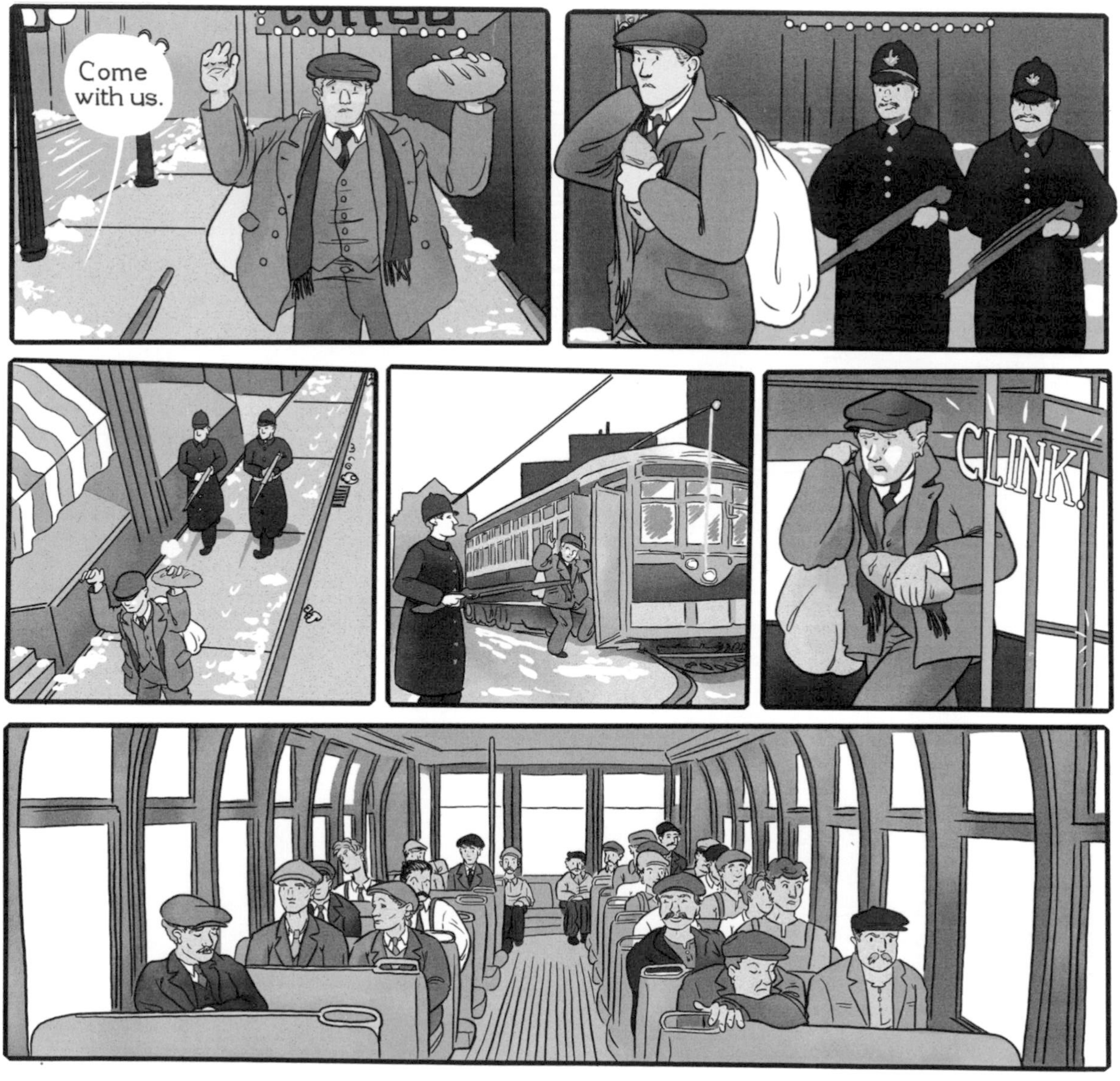
Come with us.
CLINK!

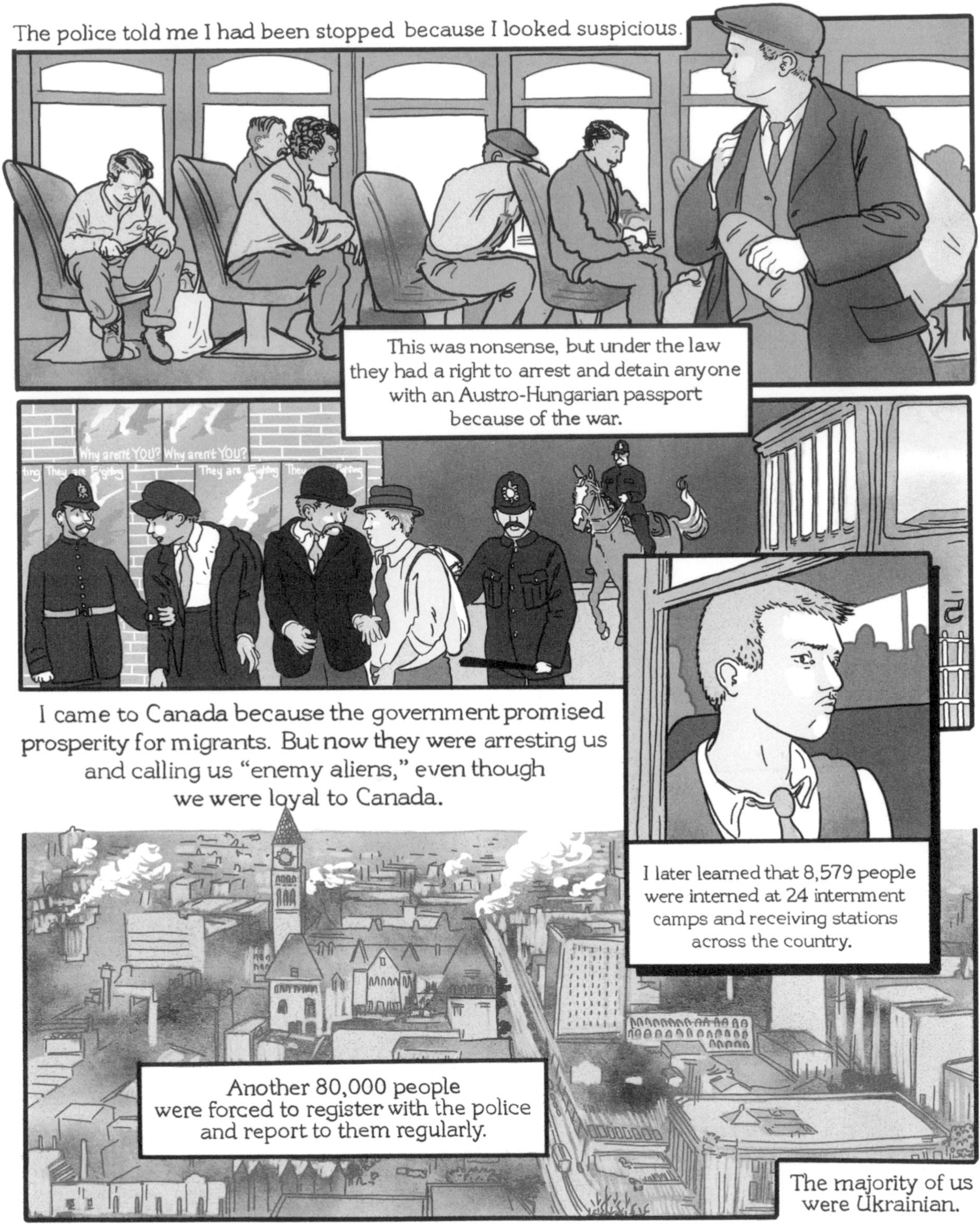
The police told me I had been stopped because I looked suspicious.
This was nonsense, but under the law they had a right to arrest and detain anyone with an Austro-Hungarian passport because of the war.
Why aren't YOU? Why aren't YOU?
They are Fighting
I came to Canada because the government promised prosperity for migrants. But now they were arresting us and calling us "enemy aliens," even though we were loyal to Canada.
I later learned that 8,579 people were interned at 24 internment camps and receiving stations across the country.
Another 80,000 people were forced to register with the police and report to them regularly.
The majority of us were Ukrainian.

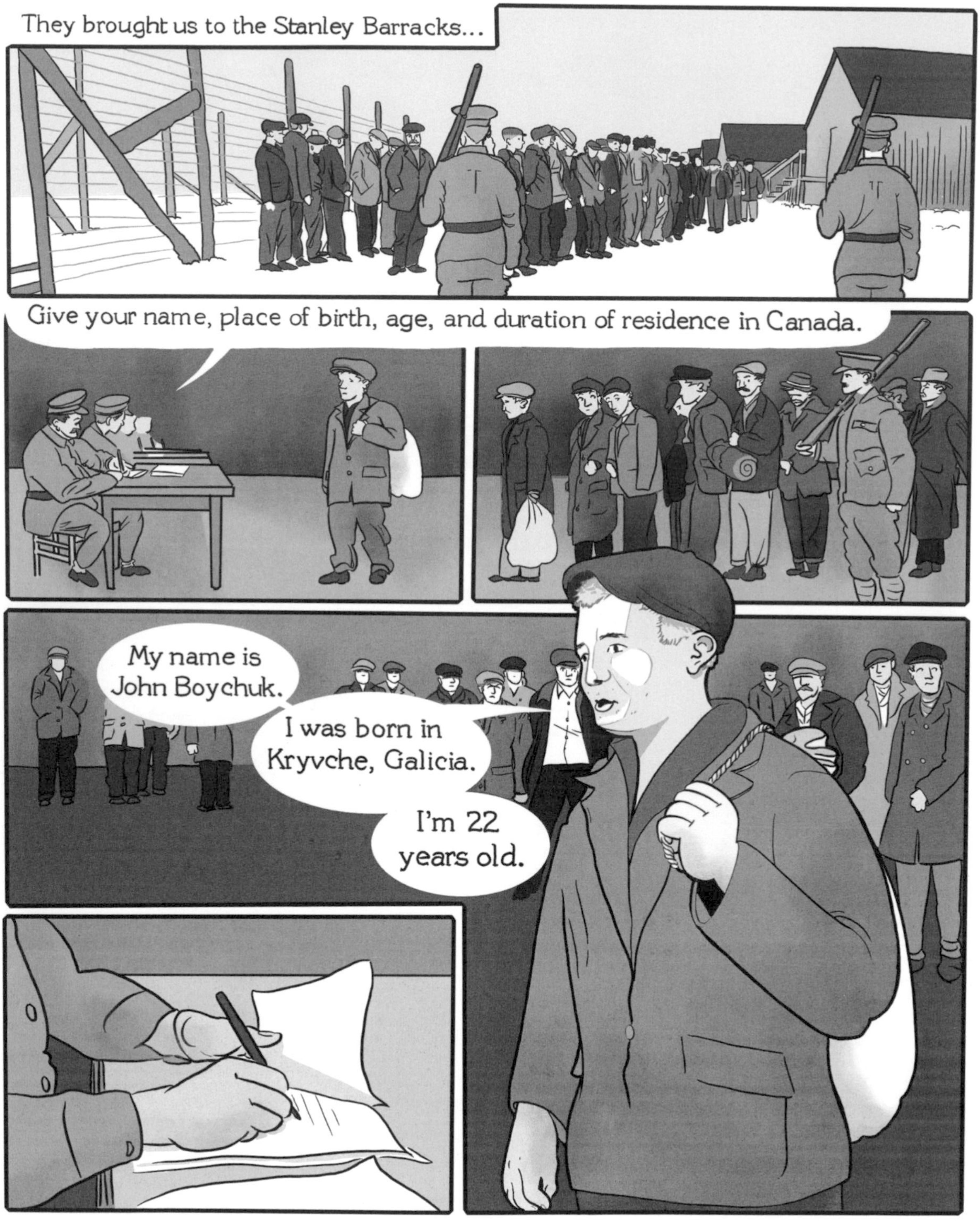
They brought us to the Stanley Barracks...
Give your name, place of birth, age, and duration of residence in Canada.
My name is John Boychuk.
I was born in Kryvche, Galicia.
I'm 22 years old.

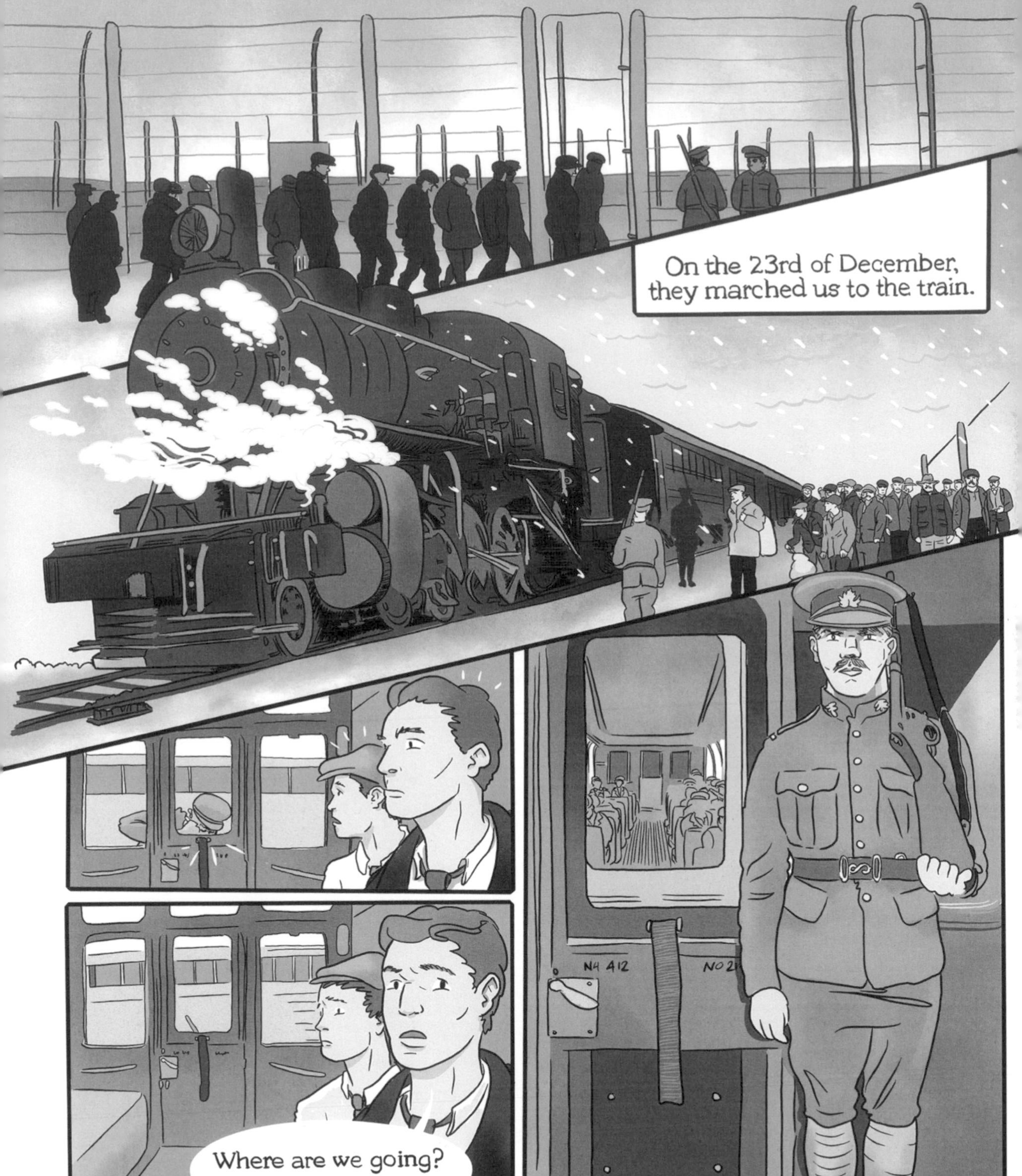
On the 23rd of December, they marched us to the train.
Where are we going?

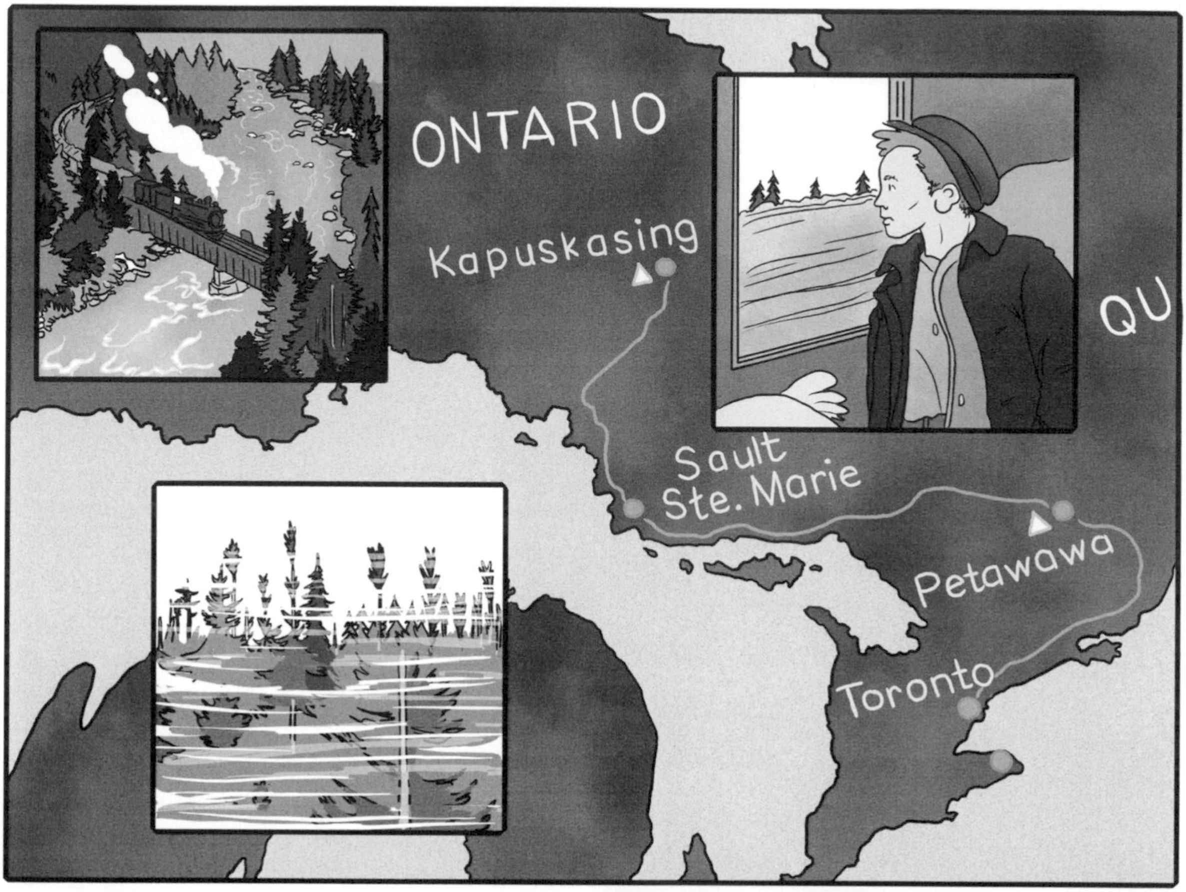
ONTARIO
Kapuskasing
QU
Sault Ste. Marie
Petawawa
Toronto

On Christmas Day, we arrived in Kapuskasing, then called MacPherson Station.

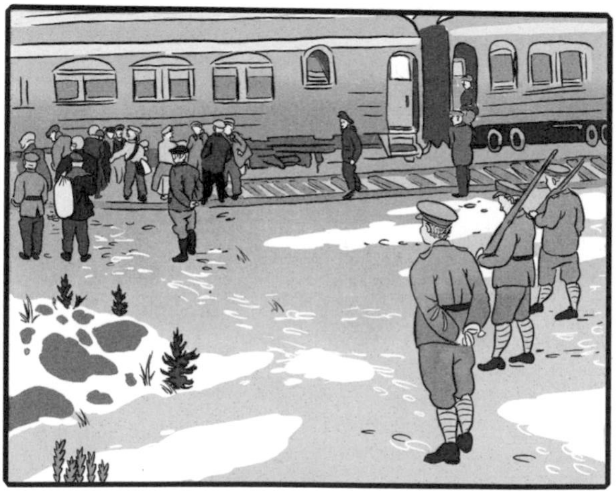

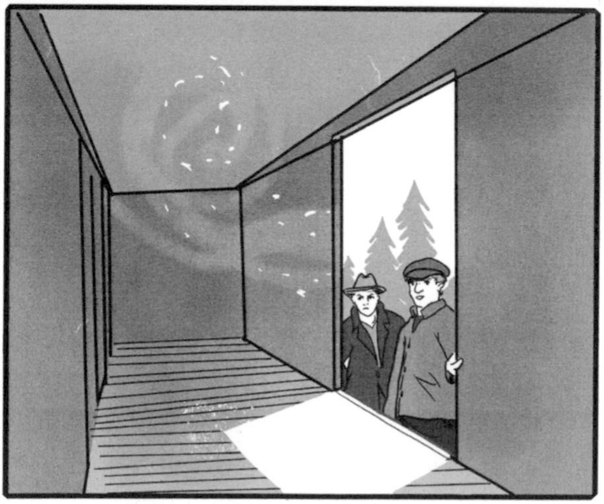

The soldiers took us to boxcars because no barracks had been built yet.

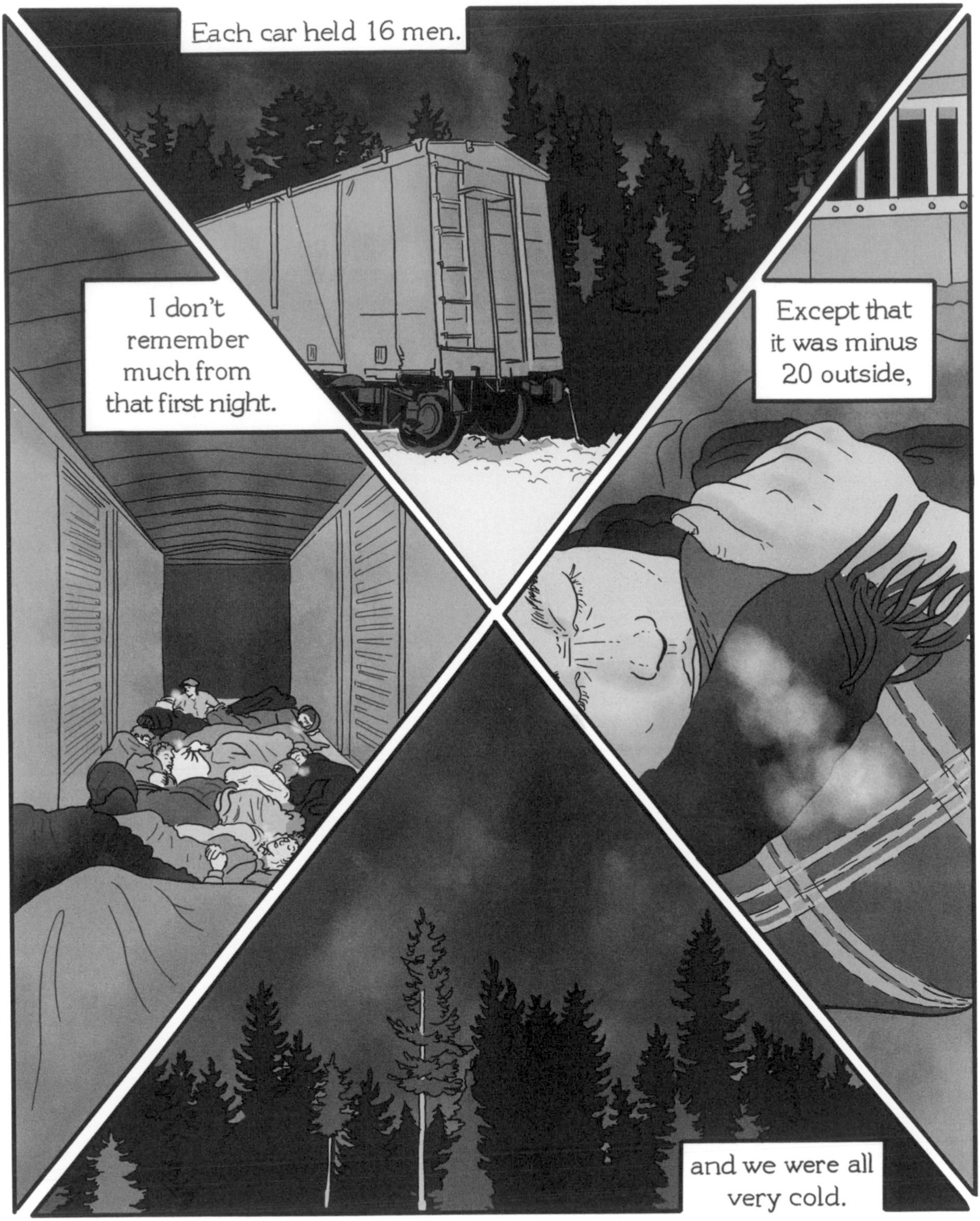
Each car held 16 men.
I don't remember much from that first night.
Except that it was minus 20 outside,
and we were all very cold.

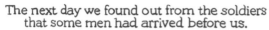

The next day we found out from the soldiers that some men had arrived before us.

They were already building two camps— one for them and one for us.

My group was tasked with building a third camp.

Take some axes and get to work, boys!

The work was brutal and exploitative.

We worked hard.
The sweat rolled down our necks only to turn chill. We were cold and hungry.

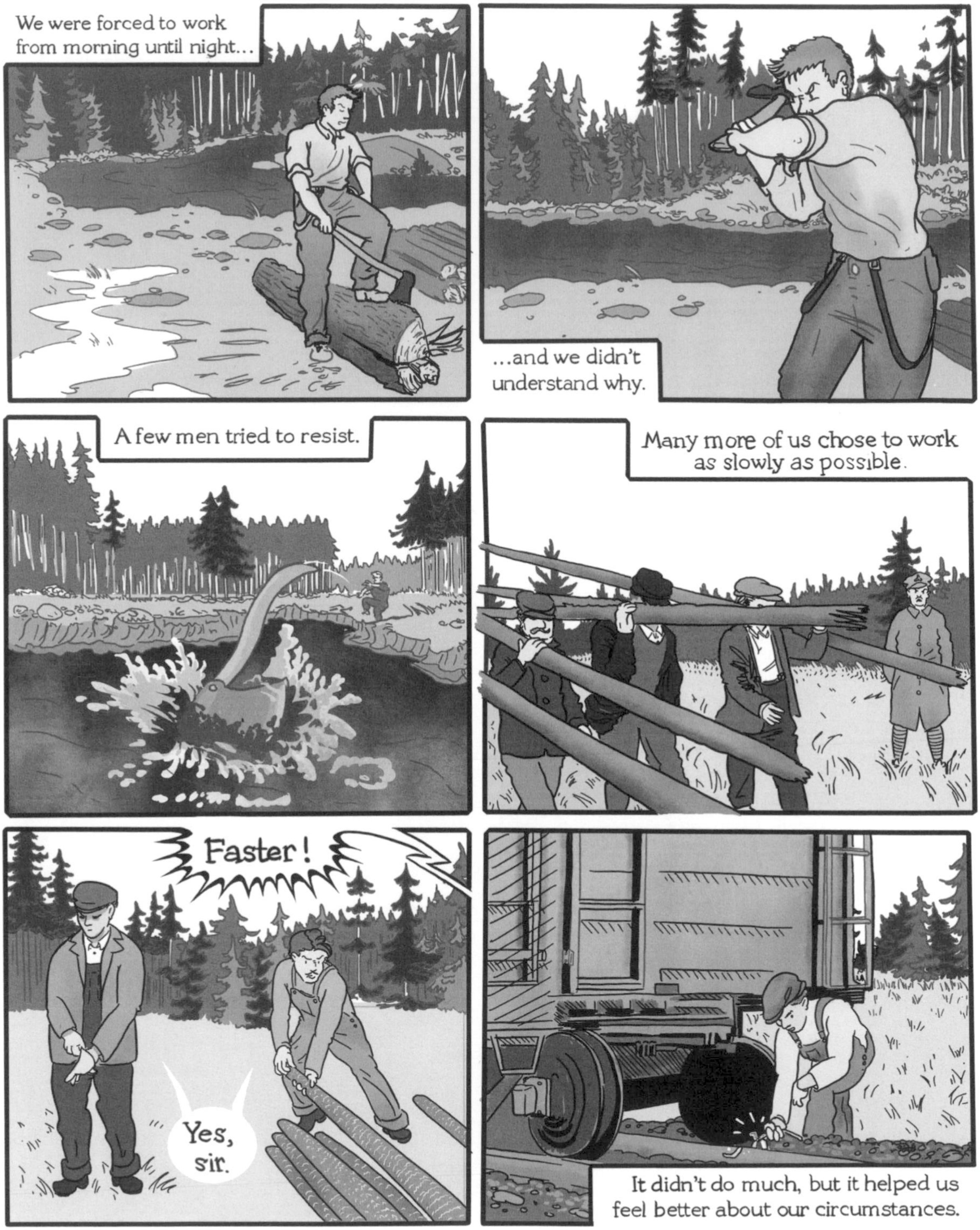
We were forced to work from morning until night...
...and we didn't understand why.
A few men tried to resist.
Many more of us chose to work as slowly as possible.
Faster!
Yes, sir.
It didn't do much, but it helped us feel better about our circumstances.

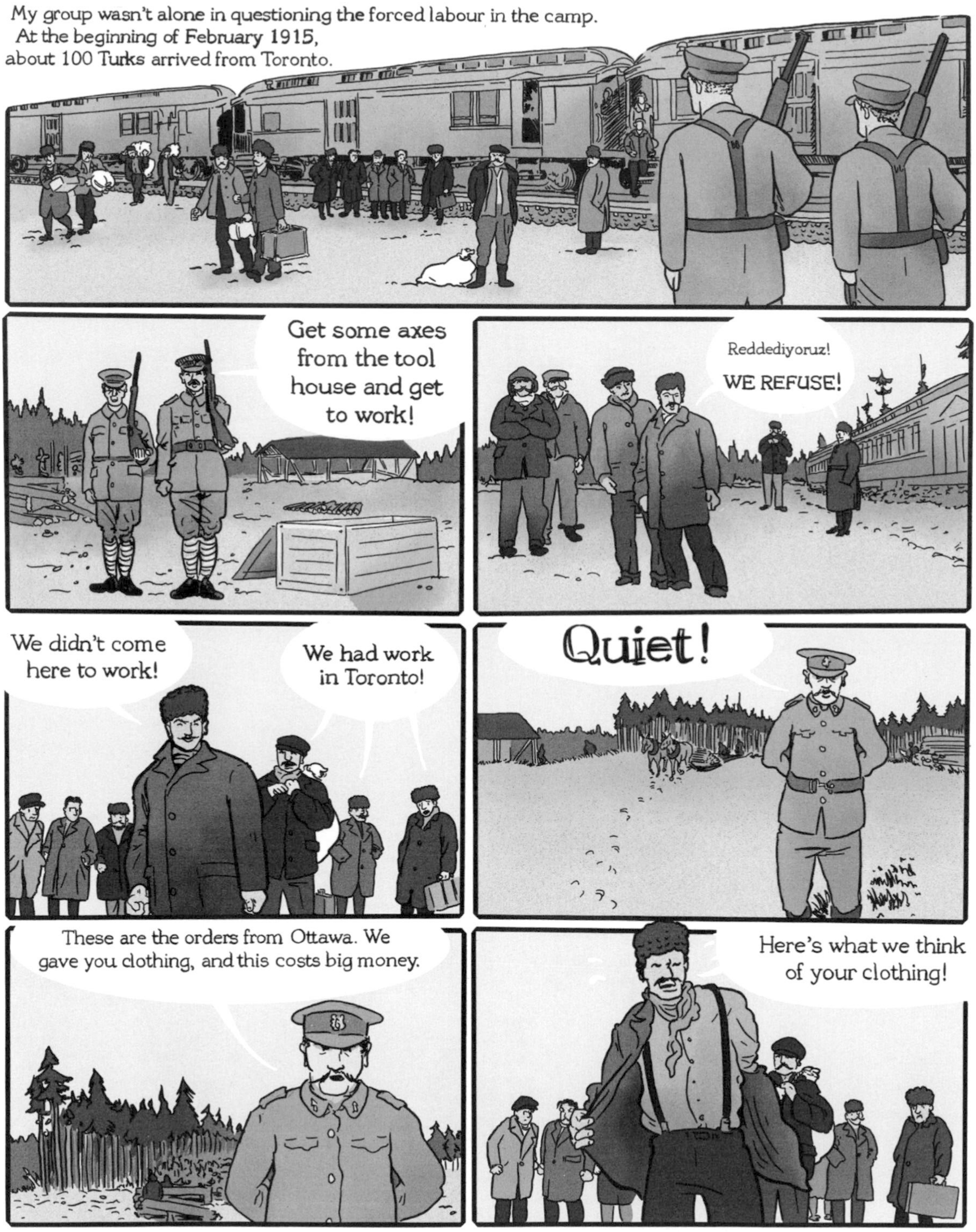
My group wasn't alone in questioning the forced labour in the camp.
At the beginning of February 1915,
about 100 Turks arrived from Toronto.
Get some axes from the tool house and get to work!
Reddediyoruz!
WE REFUSE!
We didn't come here to work!
We had work in Toronto!
Quiet!
These are the orders from Ottawa. We gave you clothing, and this costs big money.
Here's what we think of your clothing!

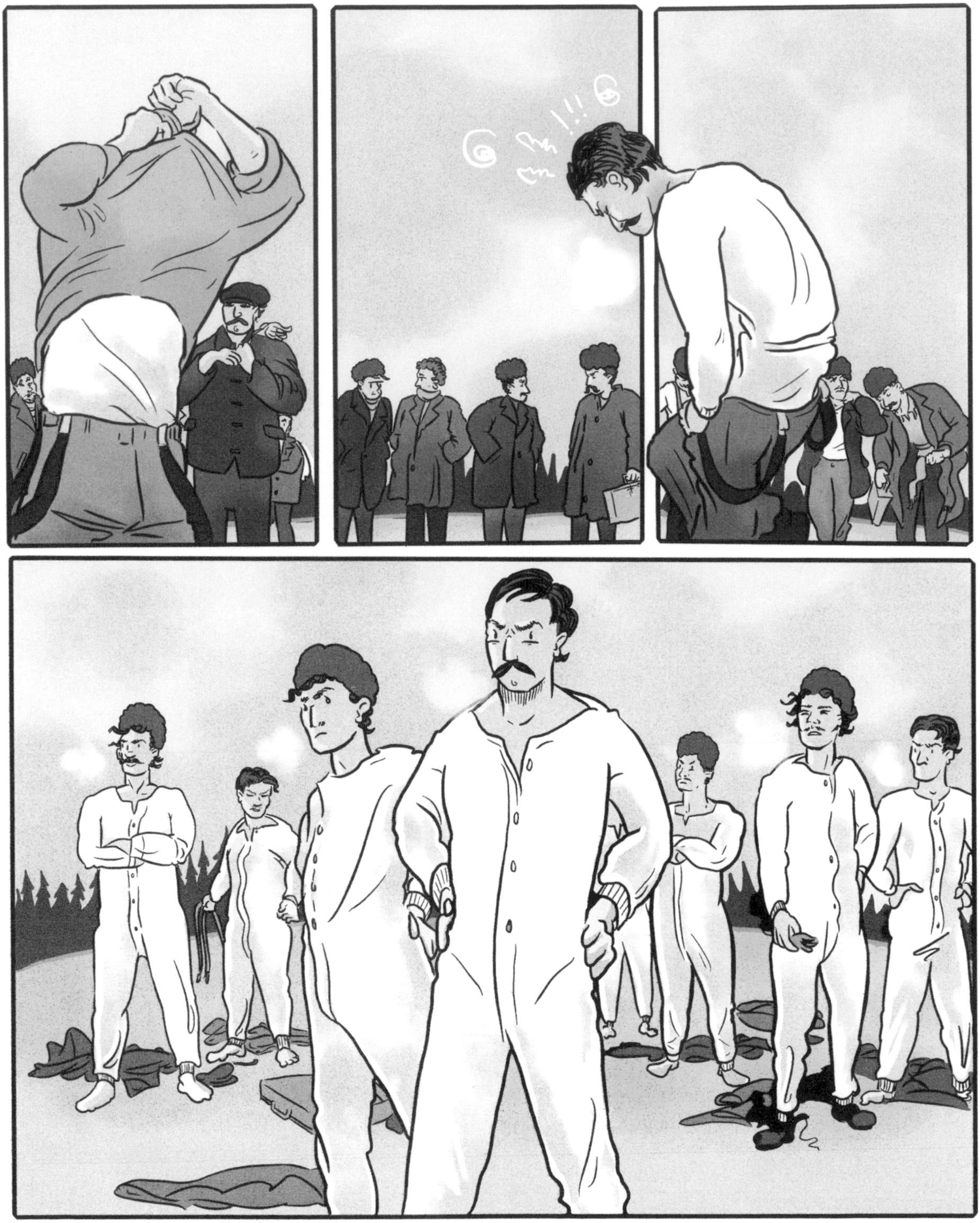

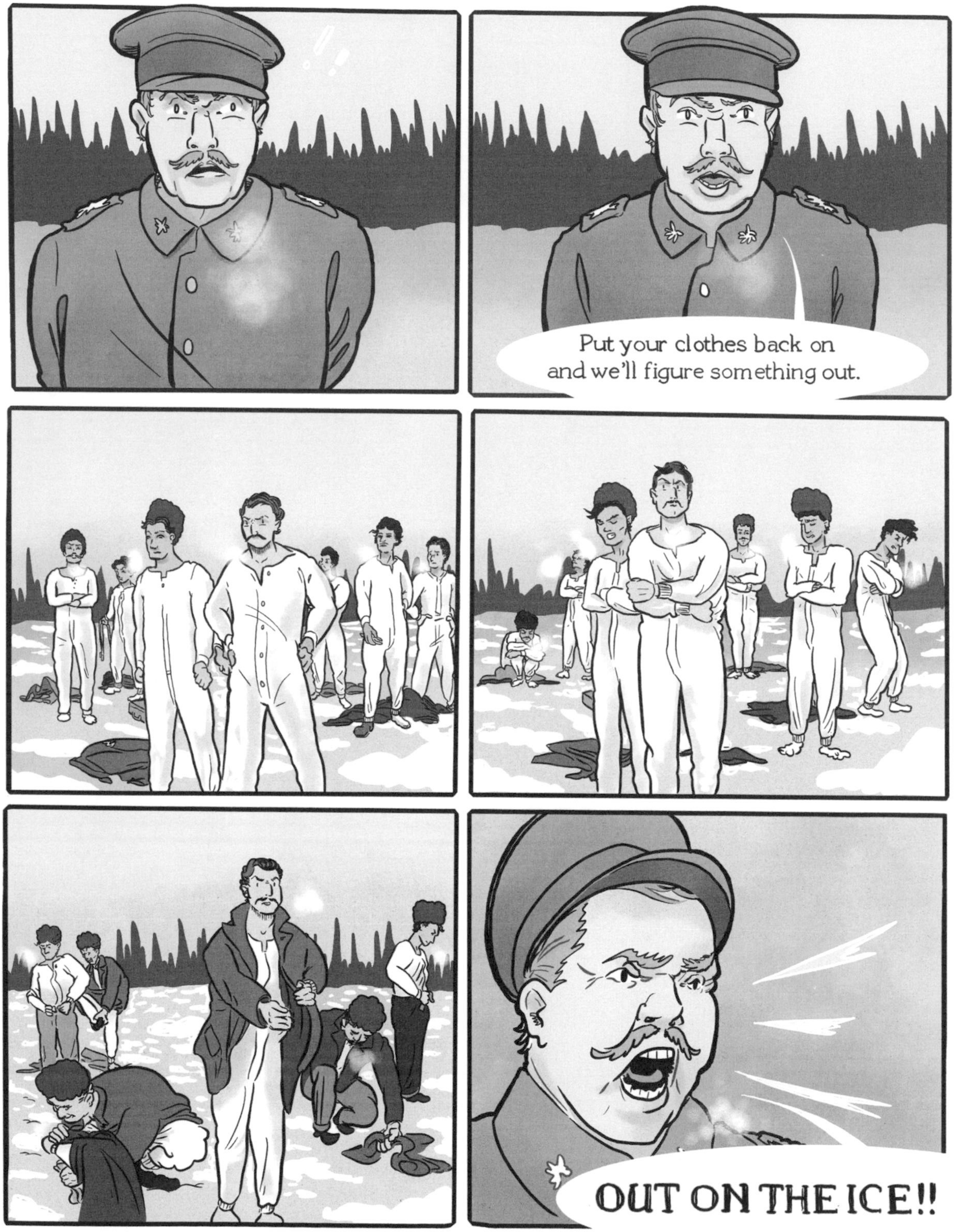

Put your clothes back on
and we'll figure something out.
OUT ON THE ICE!!

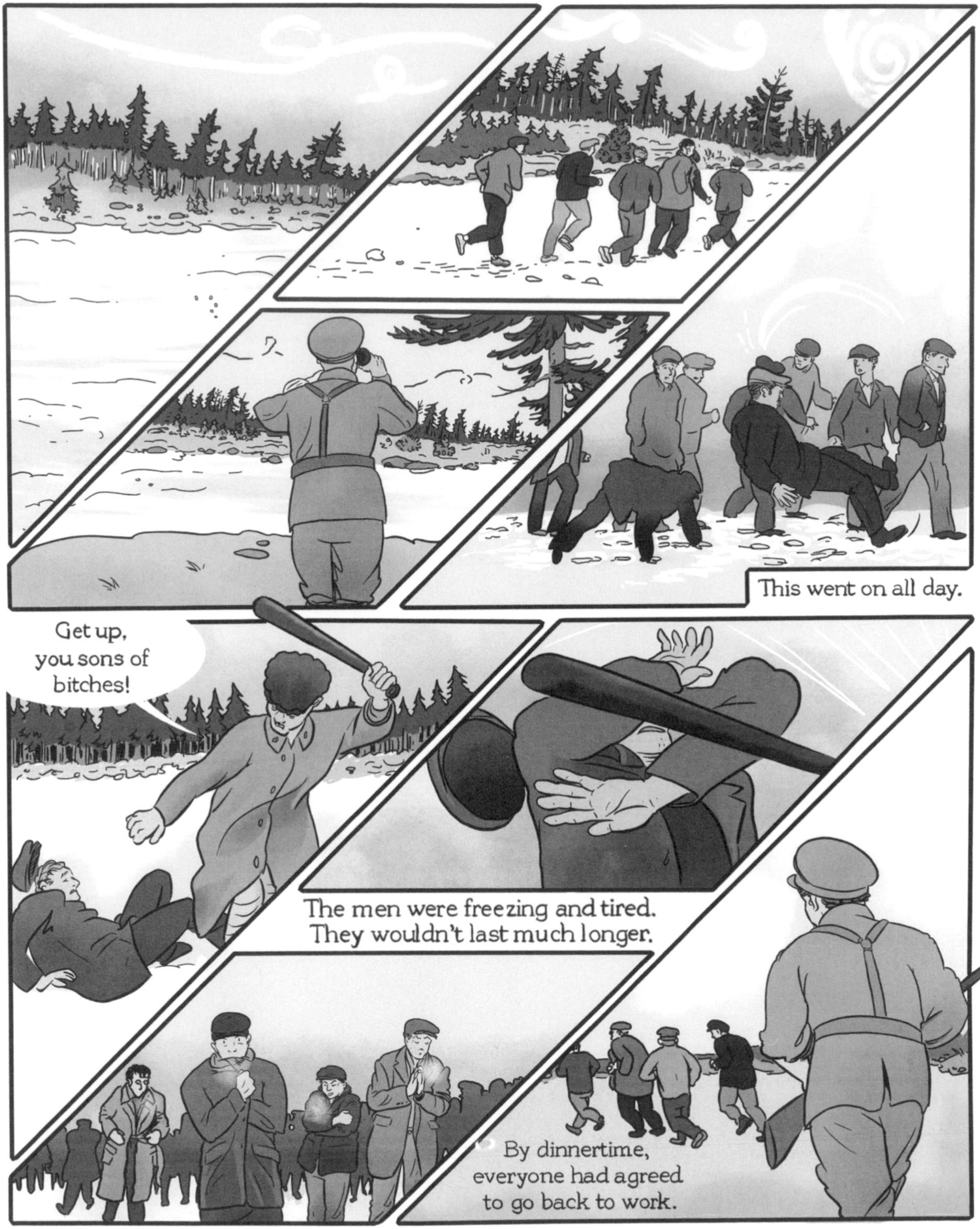
This went on all day.
Get up, you sons of bitches!
The men were freezing and tired. They wouldn't last much longer.
By dinnertime, everyone had agreed to go back to work.

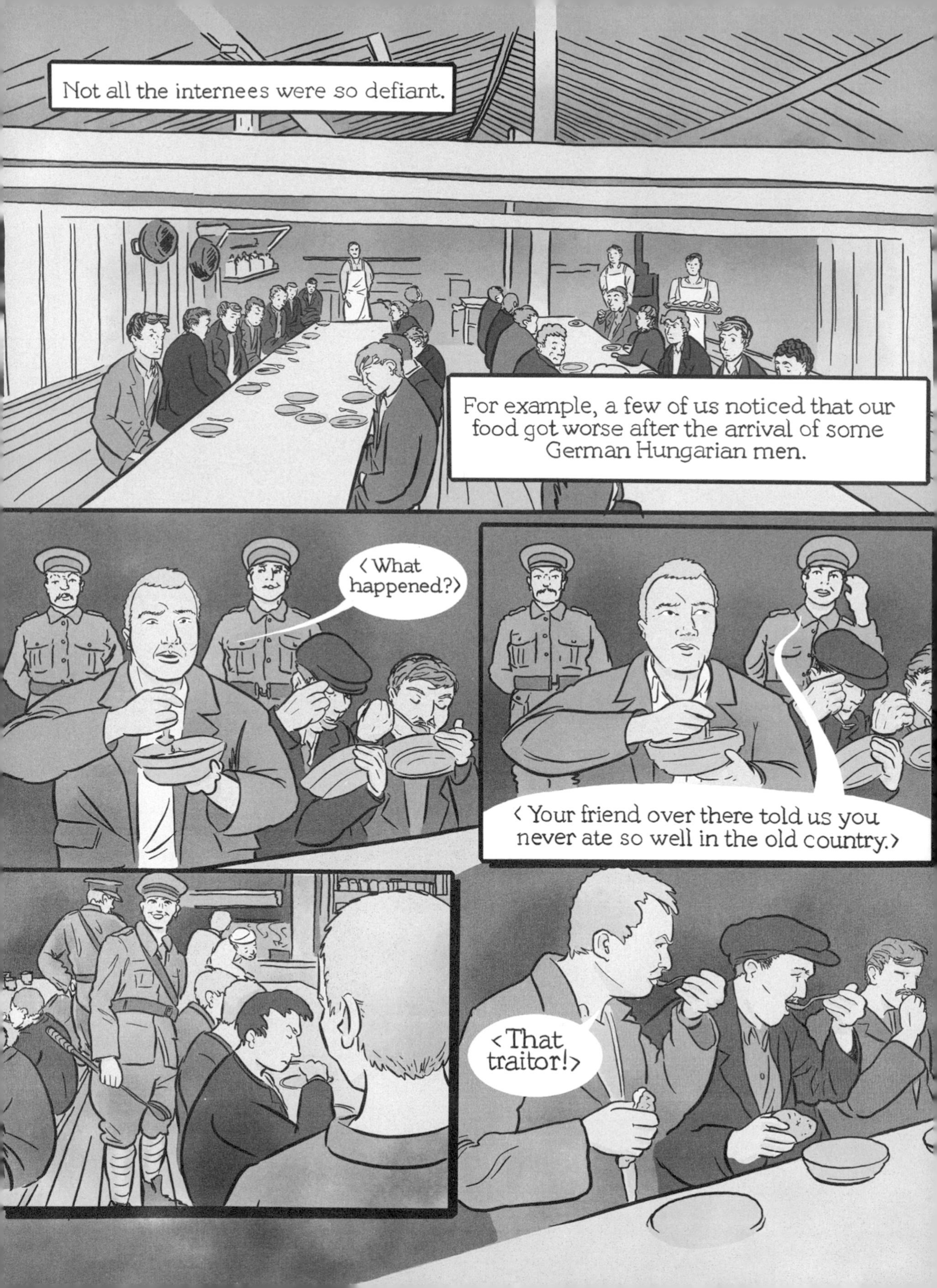
Not all the internees were so defiant.
For example, a few of us noticed that our food got worse after the arrival of some German Hungarian men.
‹What happened?›
‹Your friend over there told us you never ate so well in the old country.›
‹That traitor!›

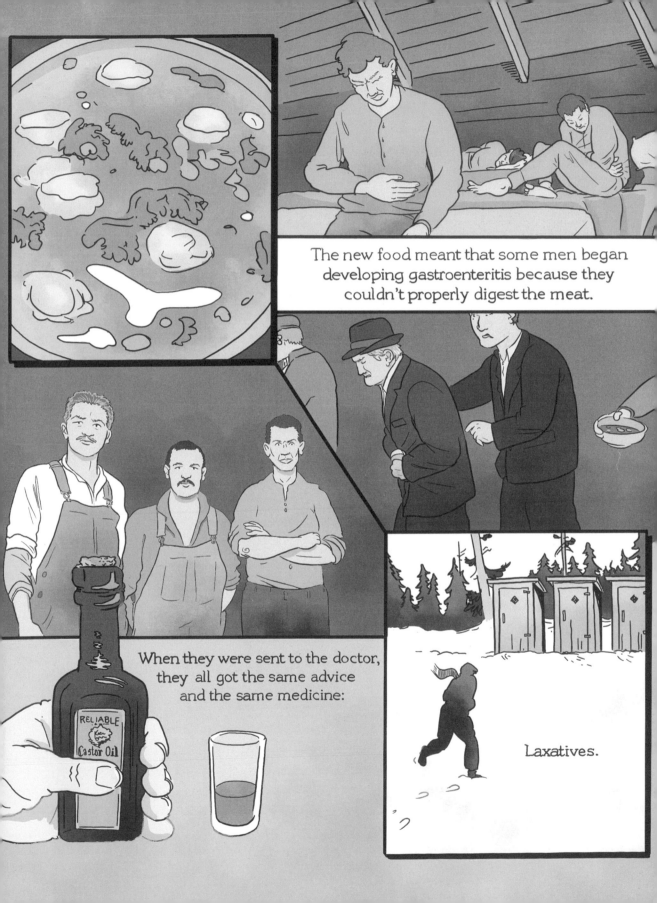

The new food meant that some men began developing gastroenteritis because they couldn't properly digest the meat.

When they were sent to the doctor, they all got the same advice and the same medicine:

Laxatives.

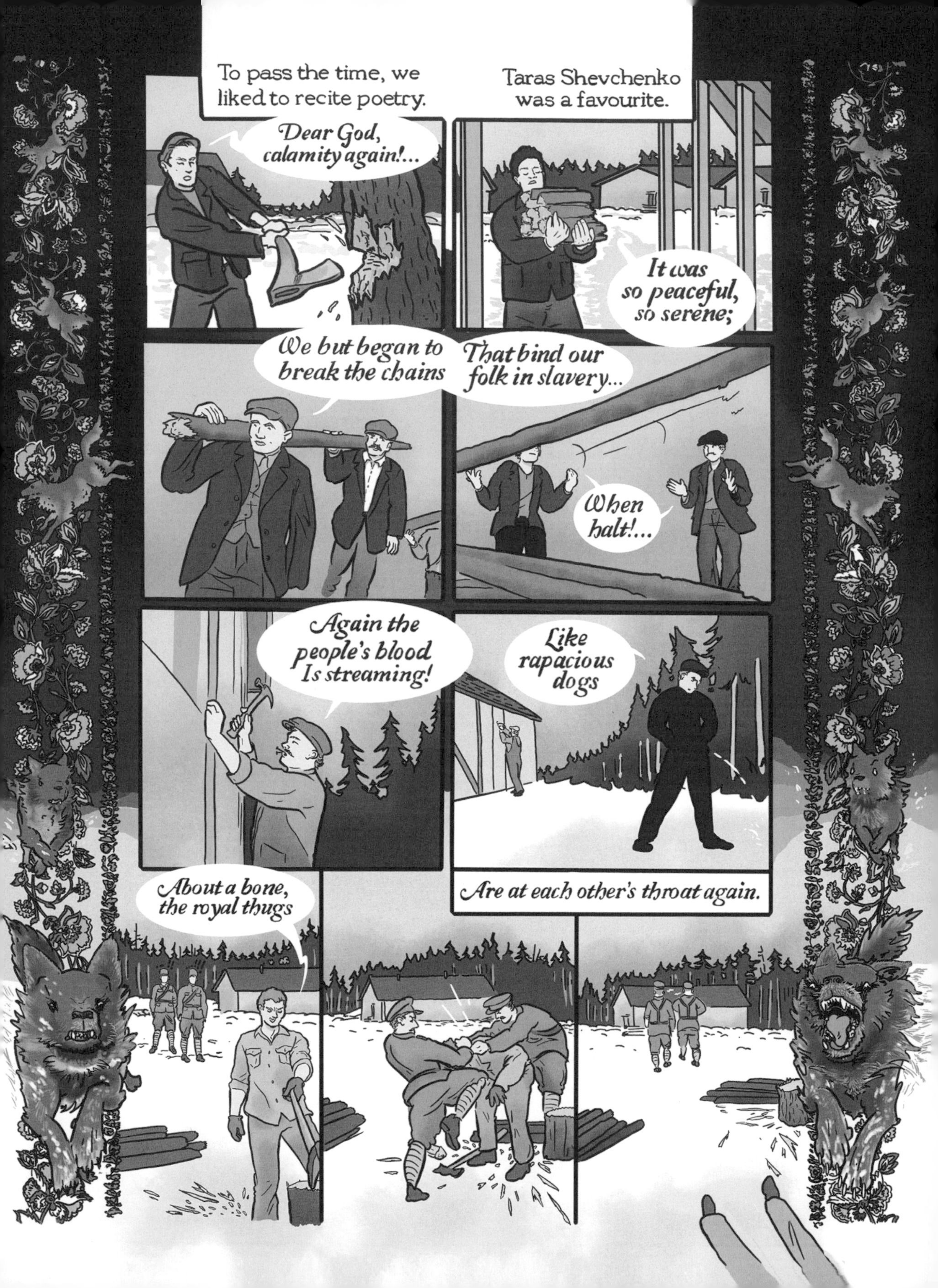

To pass the time, we liked to recite poetry.
Taras Shevchenko was a favourite.
Dear God, calamity again!...
It was so peaceful, so serene;
We but began to break the chains
That bind our folk in slavery...
When halt!...
Again the people's blood Is streaming!
Like rapacious dogs
About a bone, the royal thugs
Are at each other's throat again.

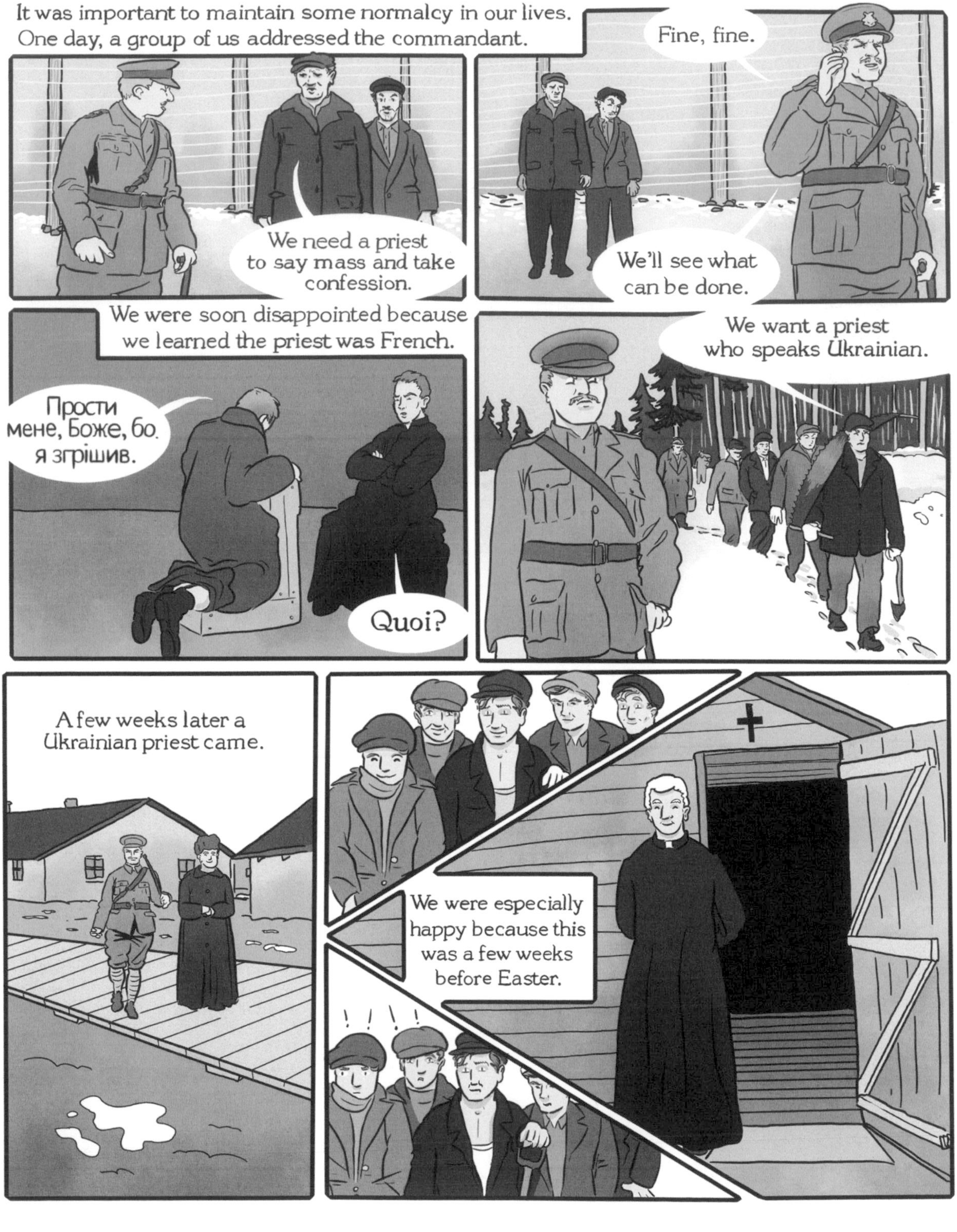
It was important to maintain some normalcy in our lives.
One day, a group of us addressed the commandant.
We need a priest to say mass and take confession.
Fine, fine.
We'll see what can be done.
We were soon disappointed because we learned the priest was French.
Прости мене, Боже, бо я згрішив.
Quoi?
We want a priest who speaks Ukrainian.
A few weeks later a Ukrainian priest came.
We were especially happy because this was a few weeks before Easter.
! ! ! !

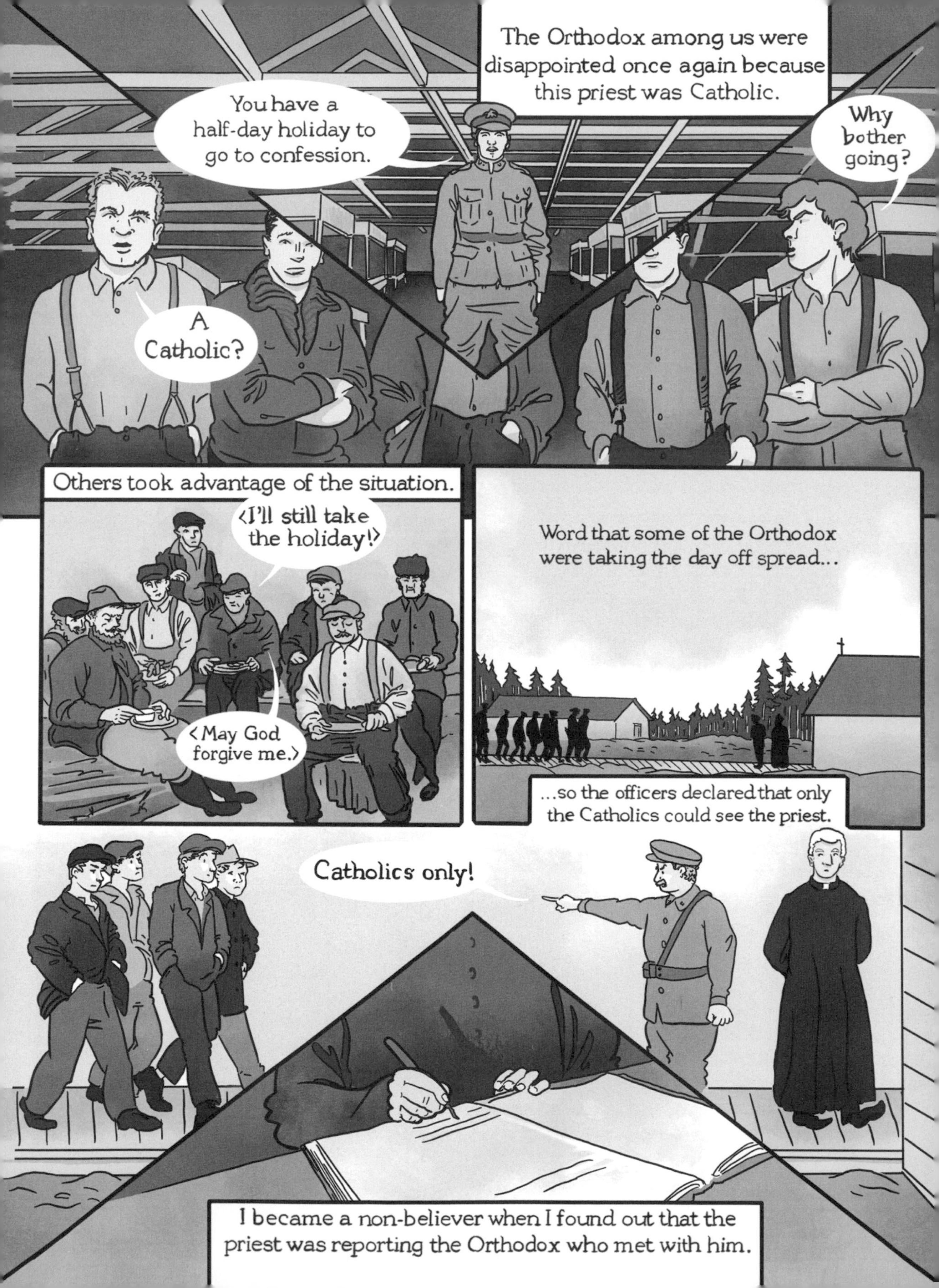
The Orthodox among us were disappointed once again because this priest was Catholic.
You have a half-day holiday to go to confession.
Why bother going?
A Catholic?
Others took advantage of the situation.
<I'll still take the holiday!>
<May God forgive me.>
Word that some of the Orthodox were taking the day off spread...
...so the officers declared that only the Catholics could see the priest.
Catholics only!
I became a non-believer when I found out that the priest was reporting the Orthodox who met with him.

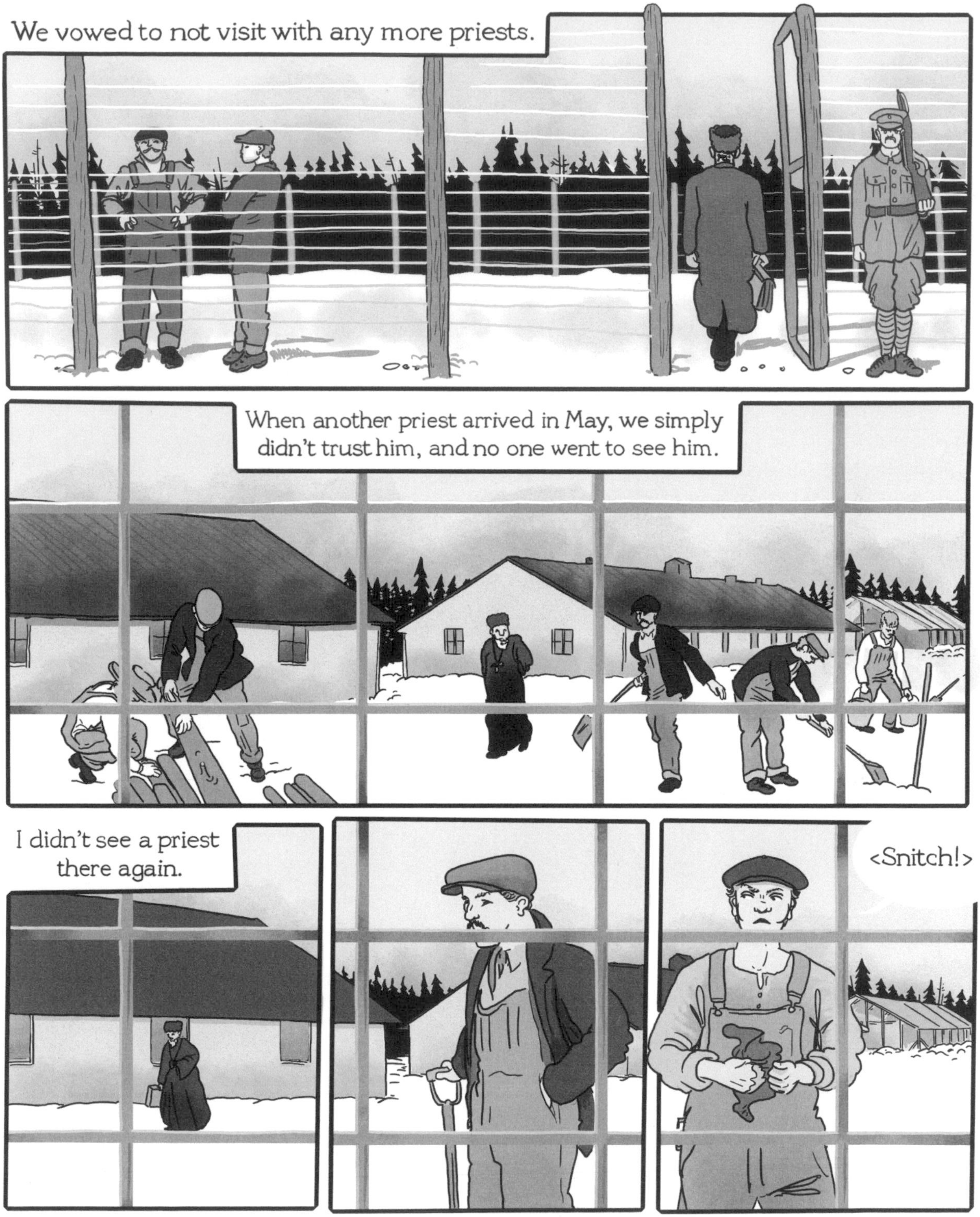
We vowed to not visit with any more priests.
When another priest arrived in May, we simply didn't trust him, and no one went to see him.
I didn't see a priest there again.
<Snitch!>

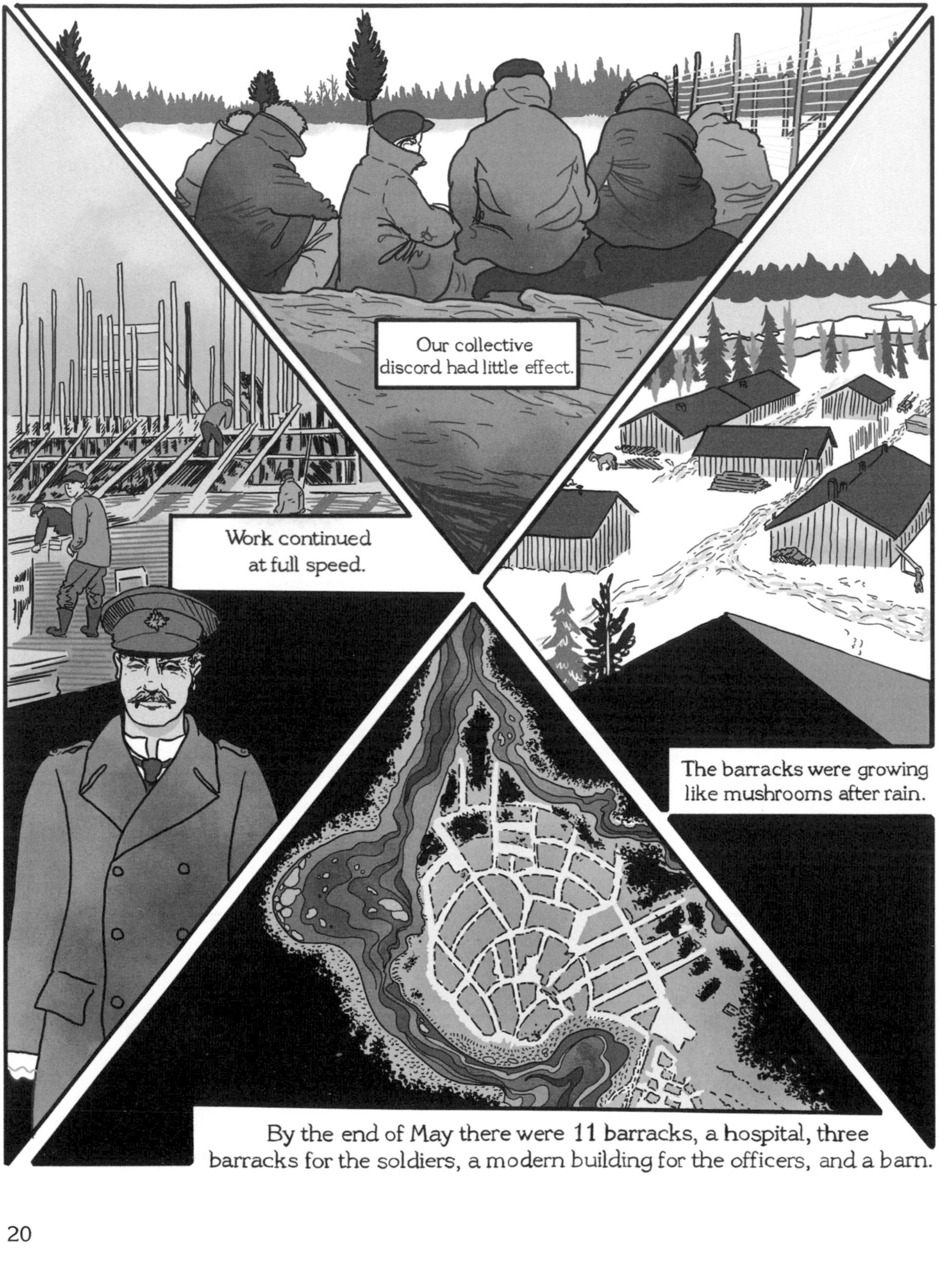
Our collective
discord had little effect.
Work continued
at full speed.
The barracks were growing
like mushrooms after rain.
By the end of May there were 11 barracks, a hospital, three
barracks for the soldiers, a modern building for the officers, and a barn.

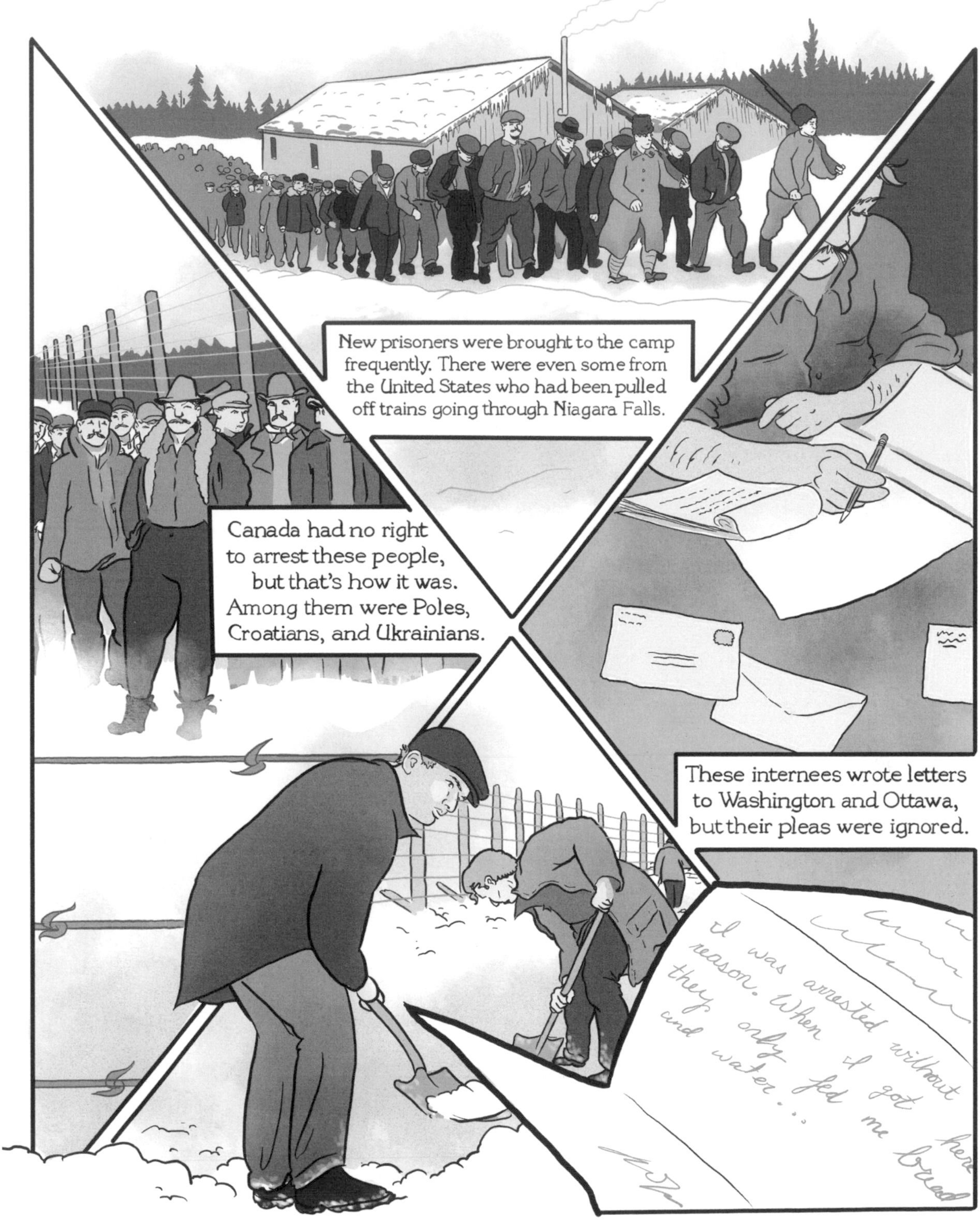
New prisoners were brought to the camp frequently. There were even some from the United States who had been pulled off trains going through Niagara Falls.
Canada had no right to arrest these people, but that's how it was. Among them were Poles, Croatians, and Ukrainians.
These internees wrote letters to Washington and Ottawa, but their pleas were ignored.
I was arrested without
reason. When I got here
they only fed me bread
and water...

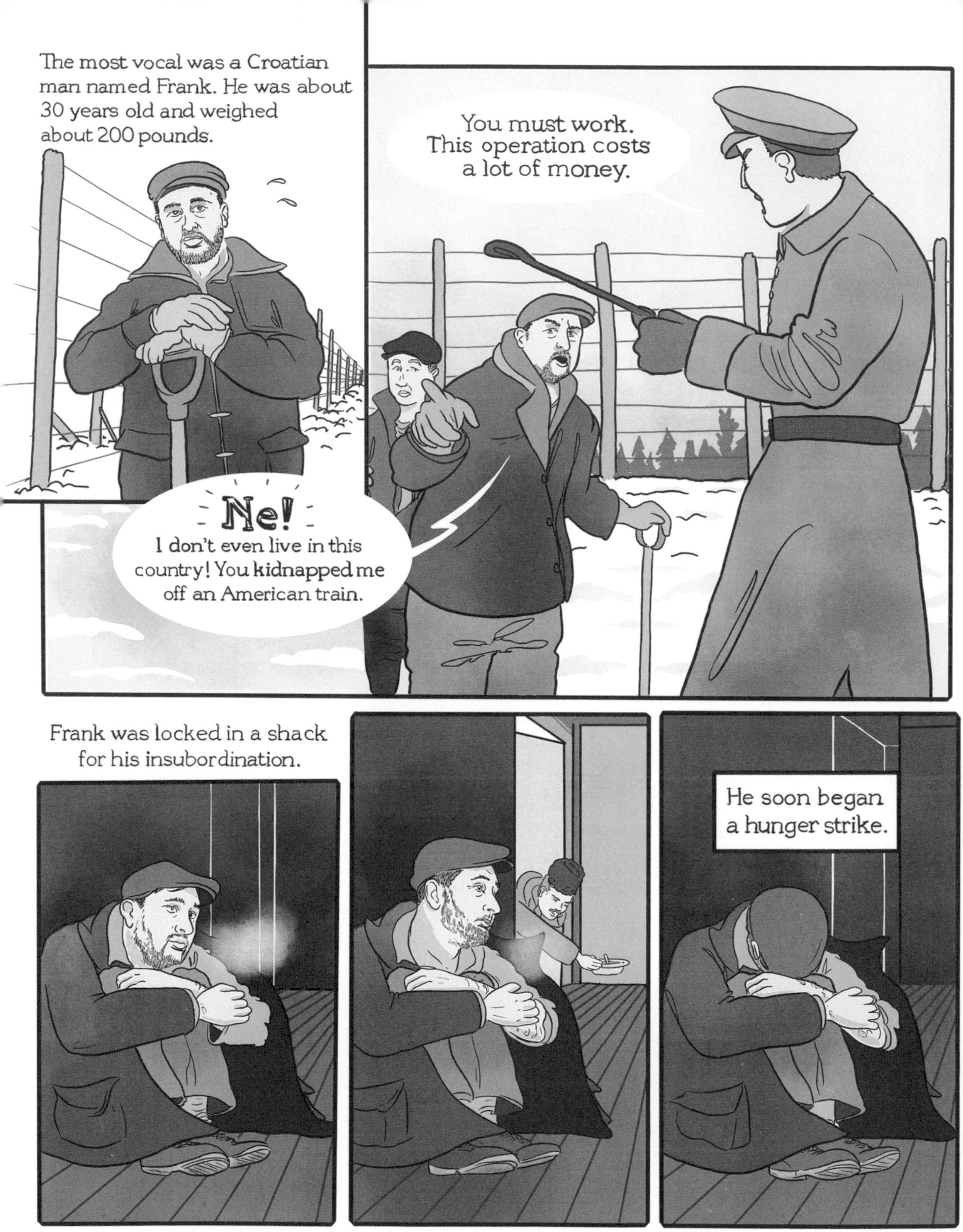
The most vocal was a Croatian man named Frank. He was about 30 years old and weighed about 200 pounds.
You must work. This operation costs a lot of money.
Ne! I don't even live in this country! You kidnapped me off an American train.
Frank was locked in a shack for his insubordination.
He soon began a hunger strike.

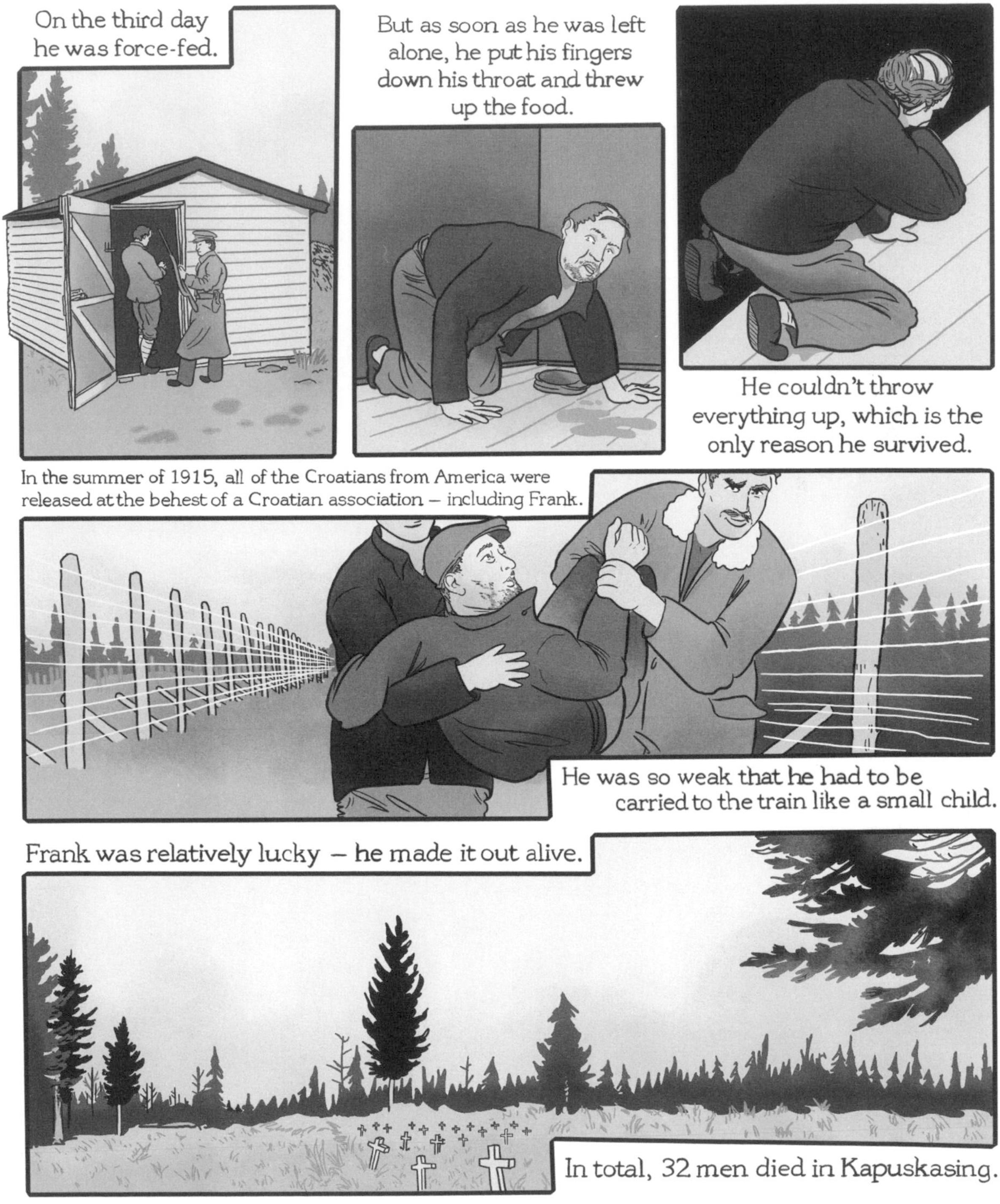
On the third day he was force-fed.
But as soon as he was left alone, he put his fingers down his throat and threw up the food.
He couldn't throw everything up, which is the only reason he survived.
In the summer of 1915, all of the Croatians from America were released at the behest of a Croatian association – including Frank.
He was so weak that he had to be carried to the train like a small child.
Frank was relatively lucky – he made it out alive.
In total, 32 men died in Kapuskasing.

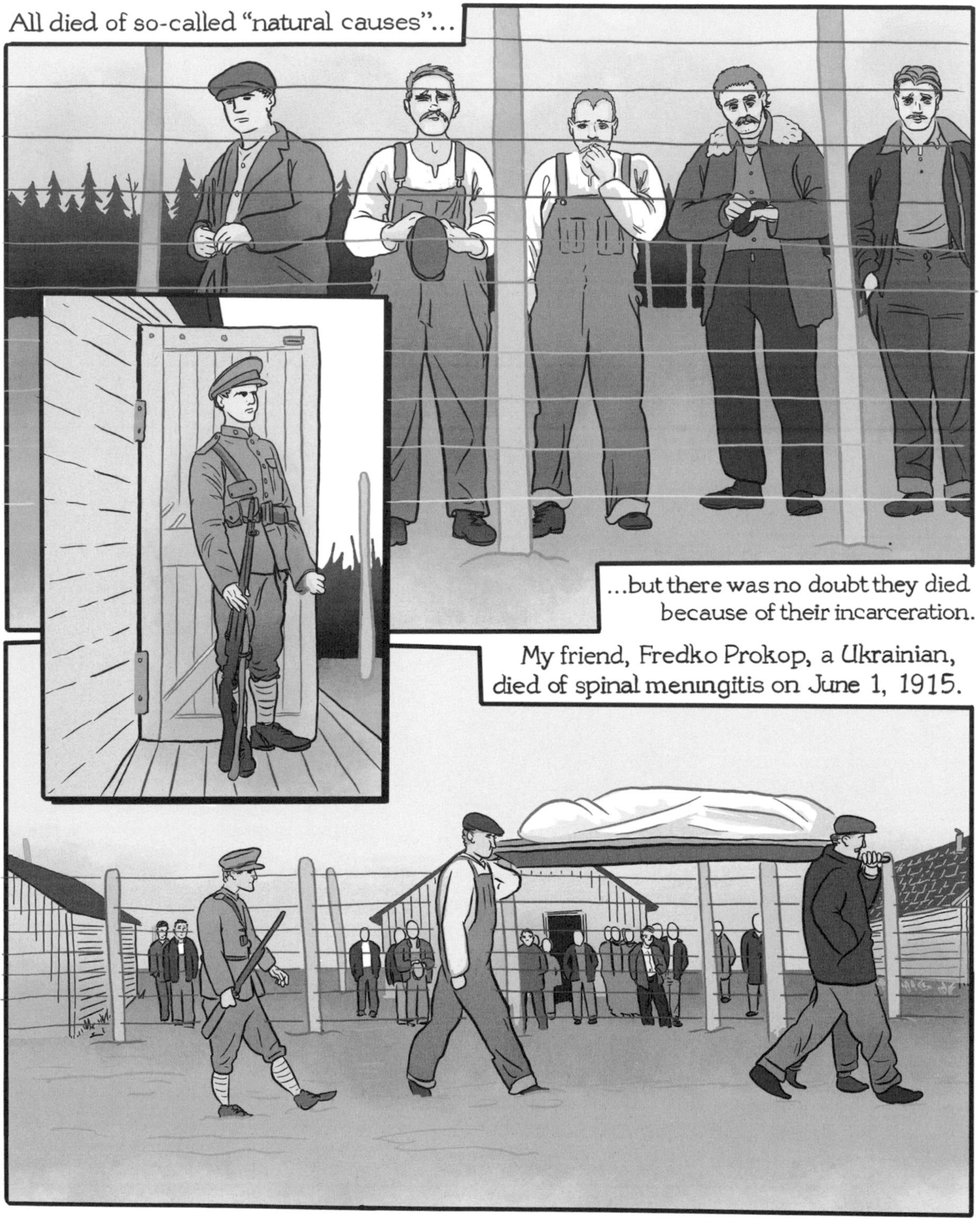
All died of so-called "natural causes"...
...but there was no doubt they died because of their incarceration.
My friend, Fredko Prokop, a Ukrainian, died of spinal meningitis on June 1, 1915.

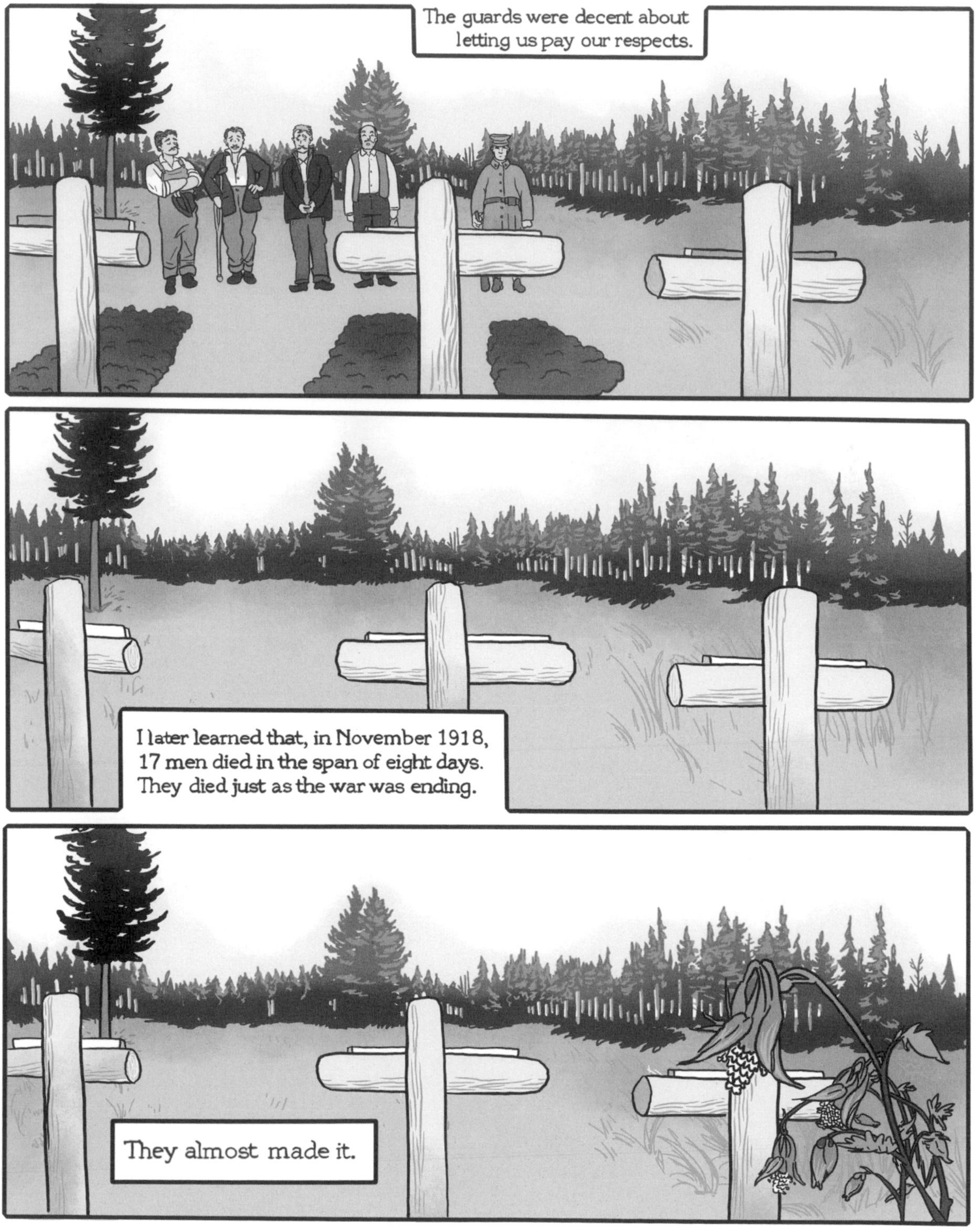
The guards were decent about letting us pay our respects.
I later learned that, in November 1918, 17 men died in the span of eight days. They died just as the war was ending.
They almost made it.

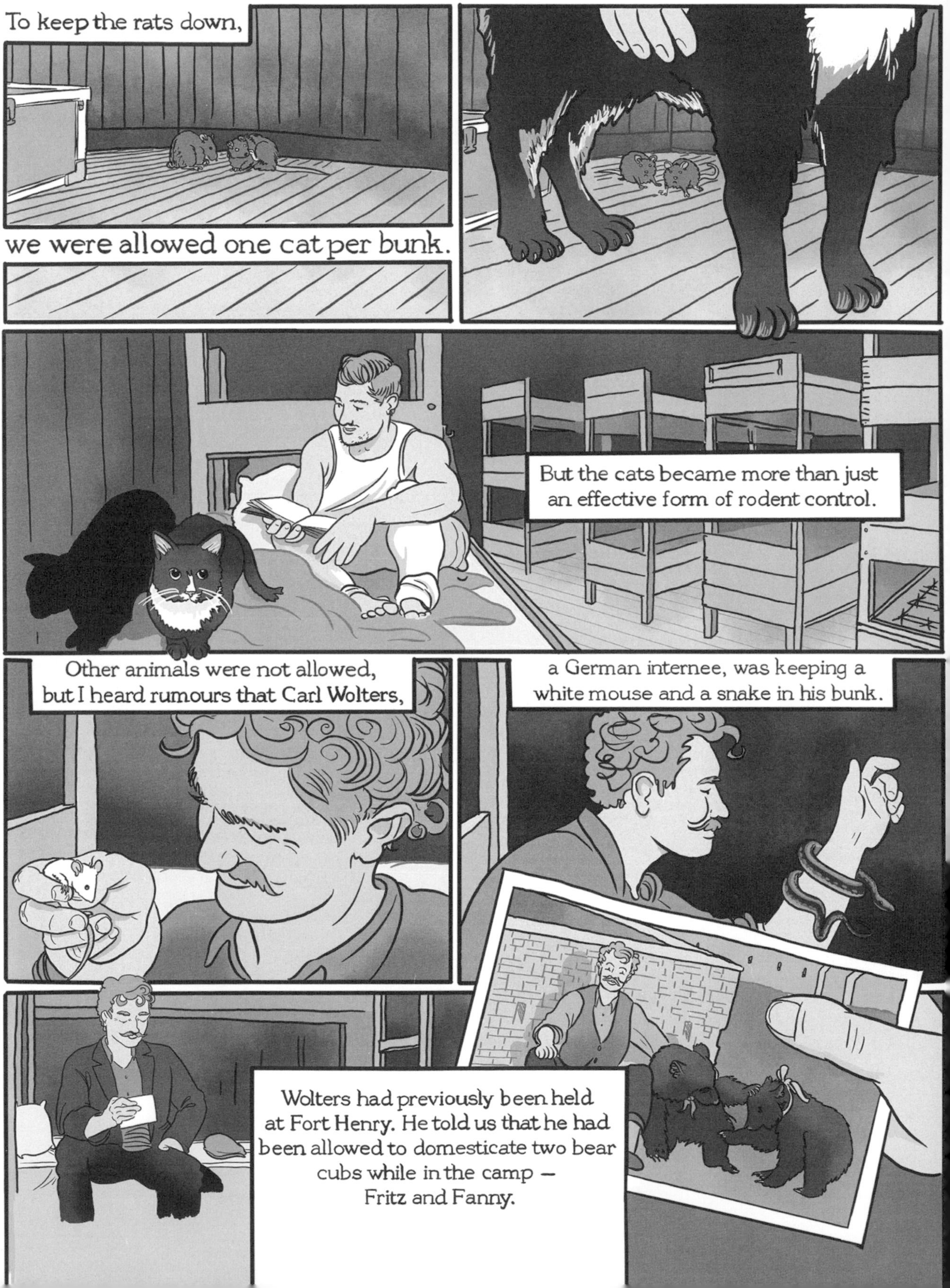
To keep the rats down,
we were allowed one cat per bunk.
But the cats became more than just an effective form of rodent control.
Other animals were not allowed, but I heard rumours that Carl Wolters,
a German internee, was keeping a white mouse and a snake in his bunk.
Wolters had previously been held at Fort Henry. He told us that he had been allowed to domesticate two bear cubs while in the camp – Fritz and Fanny.

As the war continued, industries had a labour shortage.

In the beginning of 1916, agents from various companies came to look for workers in the camps.

Hundreds of men were selected to go to various places in eastern Canada.

Many remained at the camp – including me. At first, I was upset, but then things in the camp started changing.
Upon orders from Ottawa, you have been relieved from work.
We honestly thought that things would be different now.
Austria knows about us and is looking out for us!
Aa The taxes on apples are added after
278 64 1112
278 68
4x19
The commandant even agreed to let us set up a little school for ourselves. We taught each other English and math. We were very happy with this.

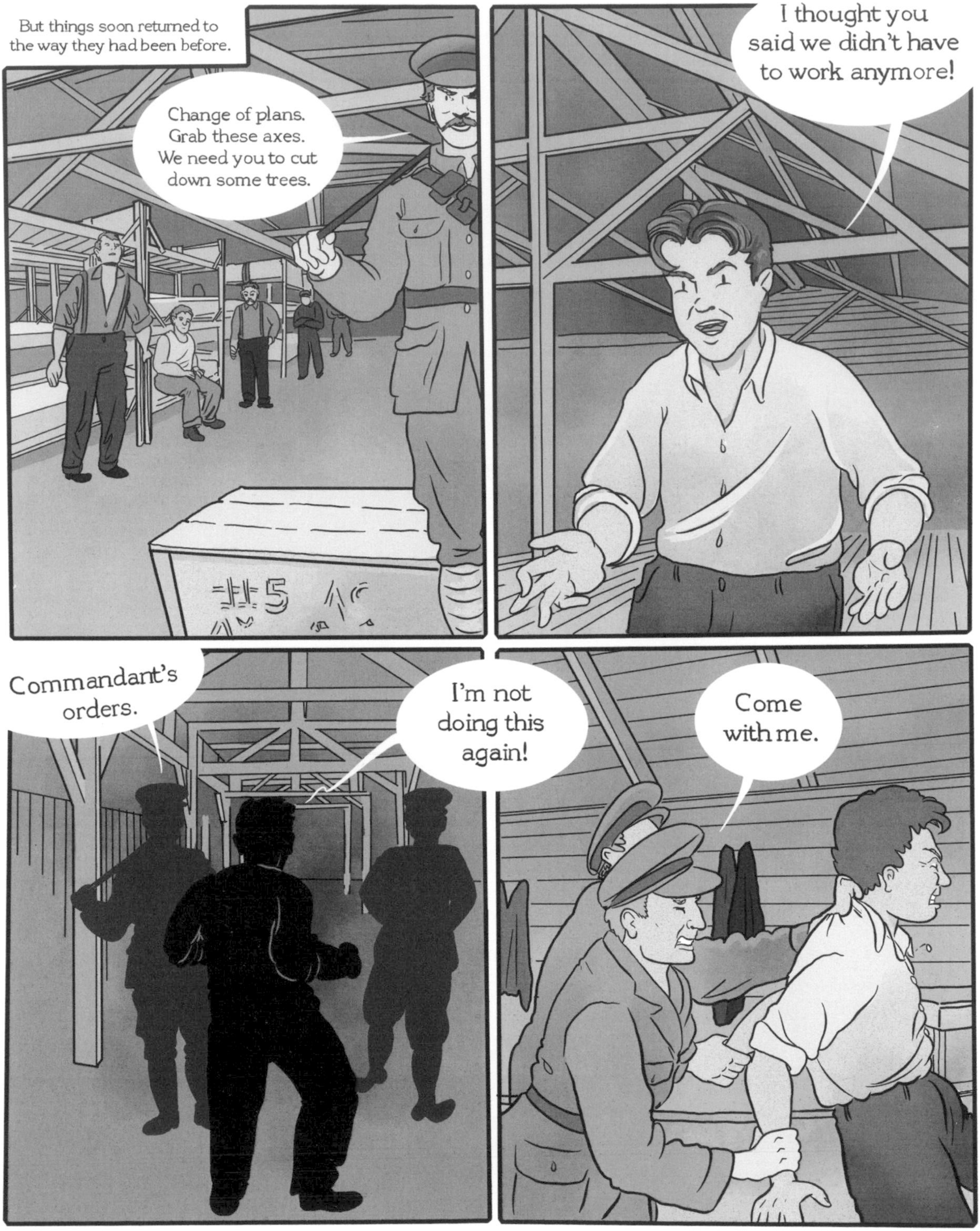
But things soon returned to the way they had been before.
Change of plans. Grab these axes. We need you to cut down some trees.
I thought you said we didn't have to work anymore!
Commandant's orders.
I'm not doing this again!
Come with me.

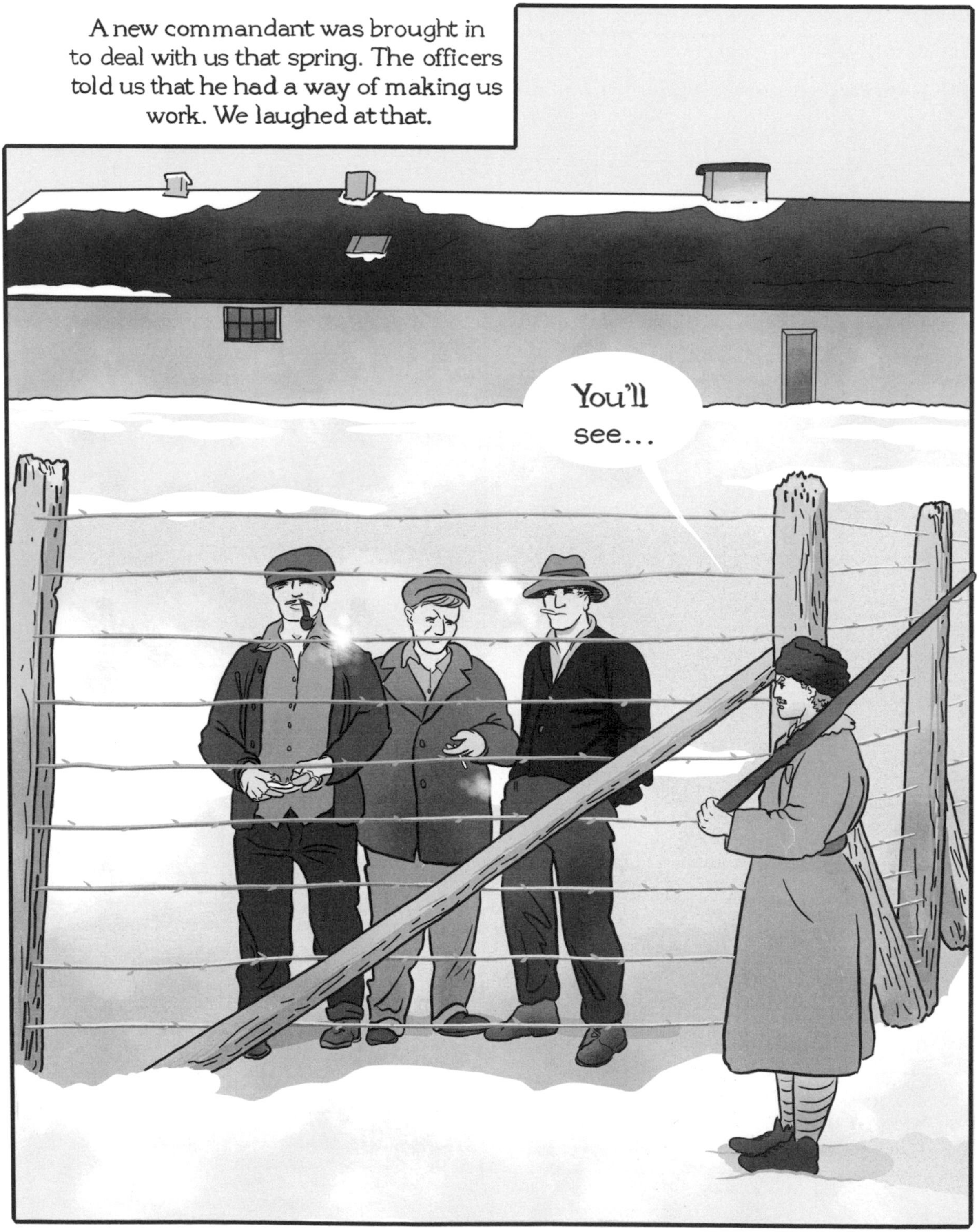
A new commandant was brought in to deal with us that spring. The officers told us that he had a way of making us work. We laughed at that.
You'll see...

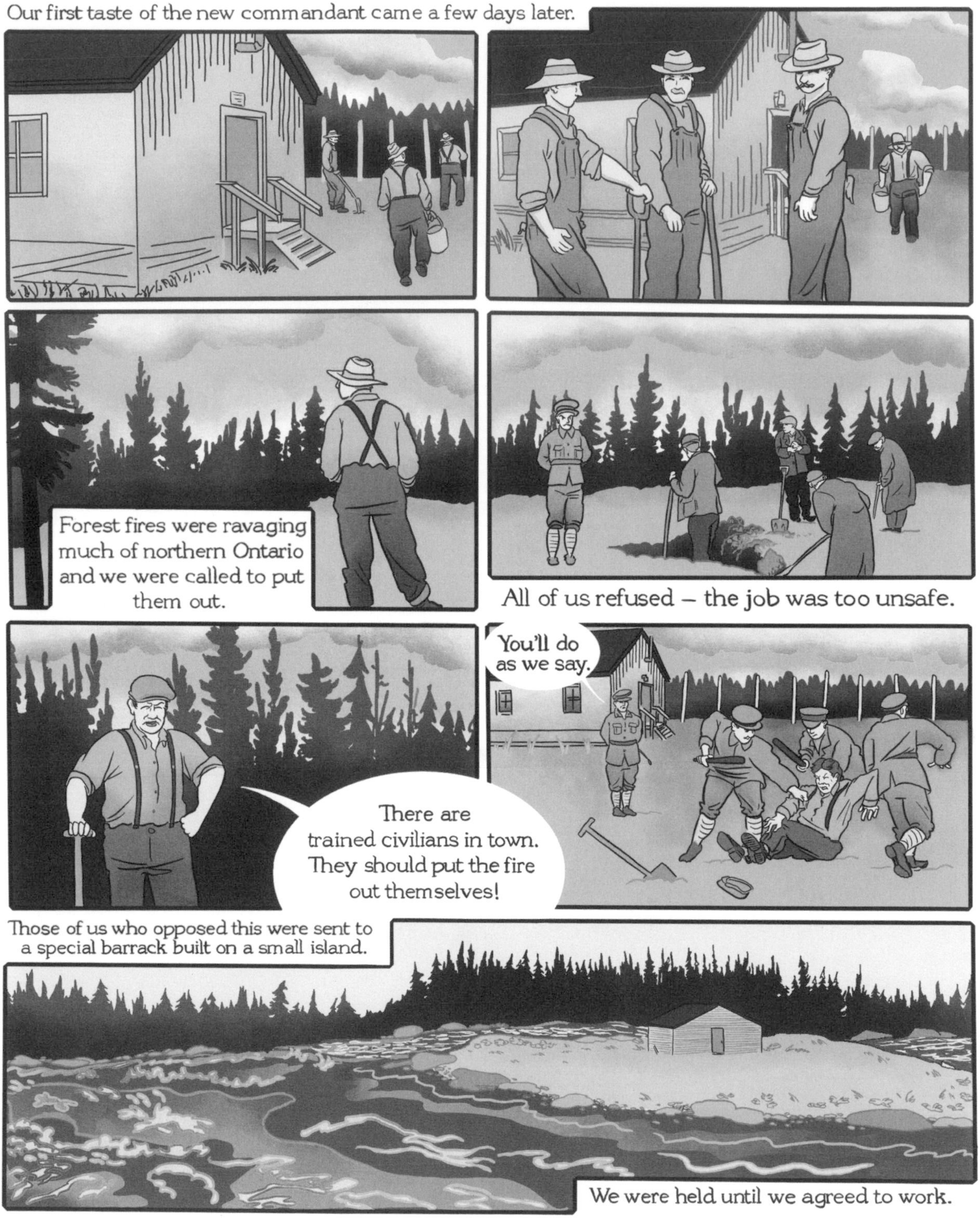
Our first taste of the new commandant came a few days later.
Forest fires were ravaging much of northern Ontario and we were called to put them out.
All of us refused – the job was too unsafe.
There are trained civilians in town. They should put the fire out themselves!
You'll do as we say.
Those of us who opposed this were sent to a special barrack built on a small island.
We were held until we agreed to work.

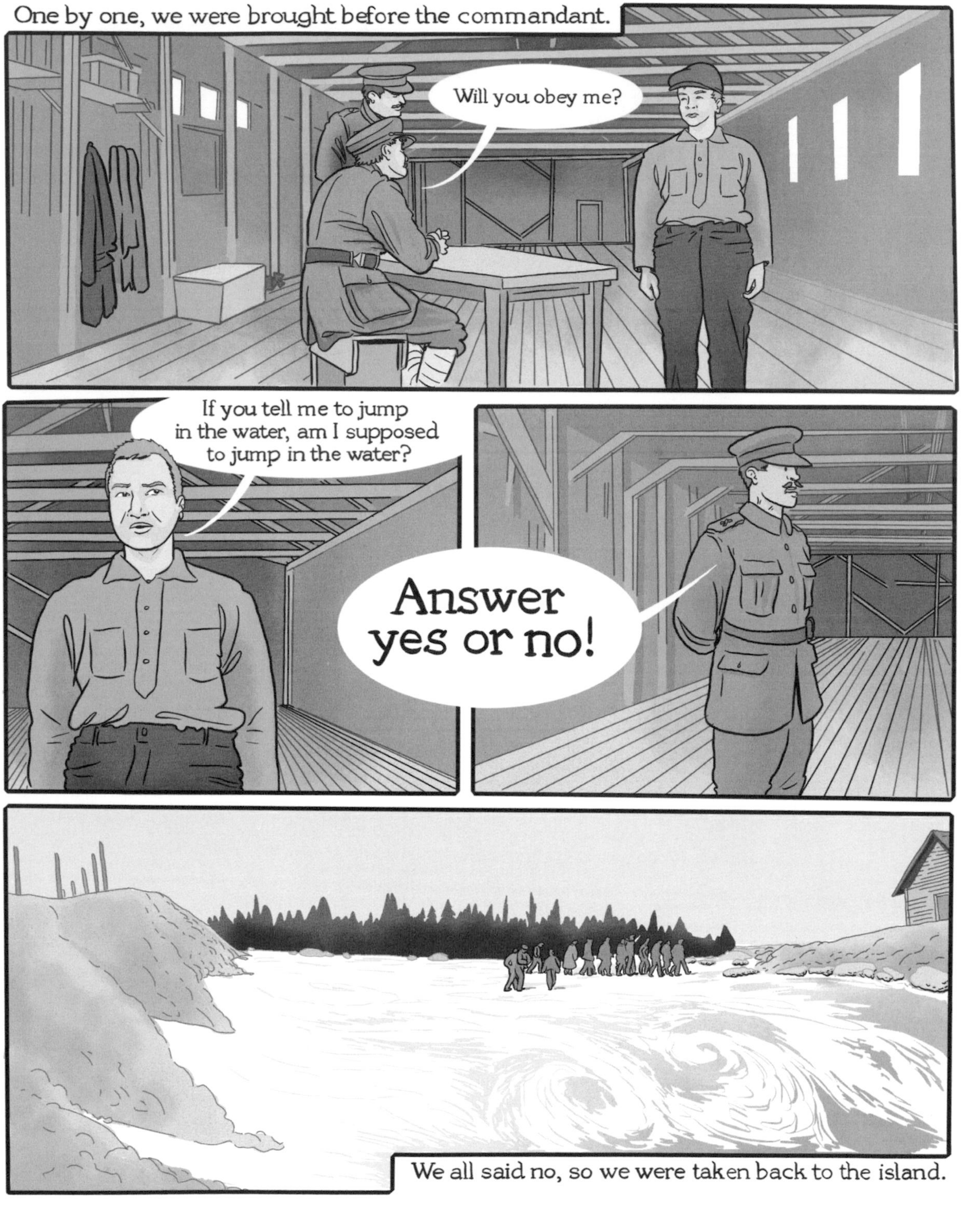
One by one, we were brought before the commandant.
Will you obey me?
If you tell me to jump in the water, am I supposed to jump in the water?
Answer yes or no!
We all said no, so we were taken back to the island.

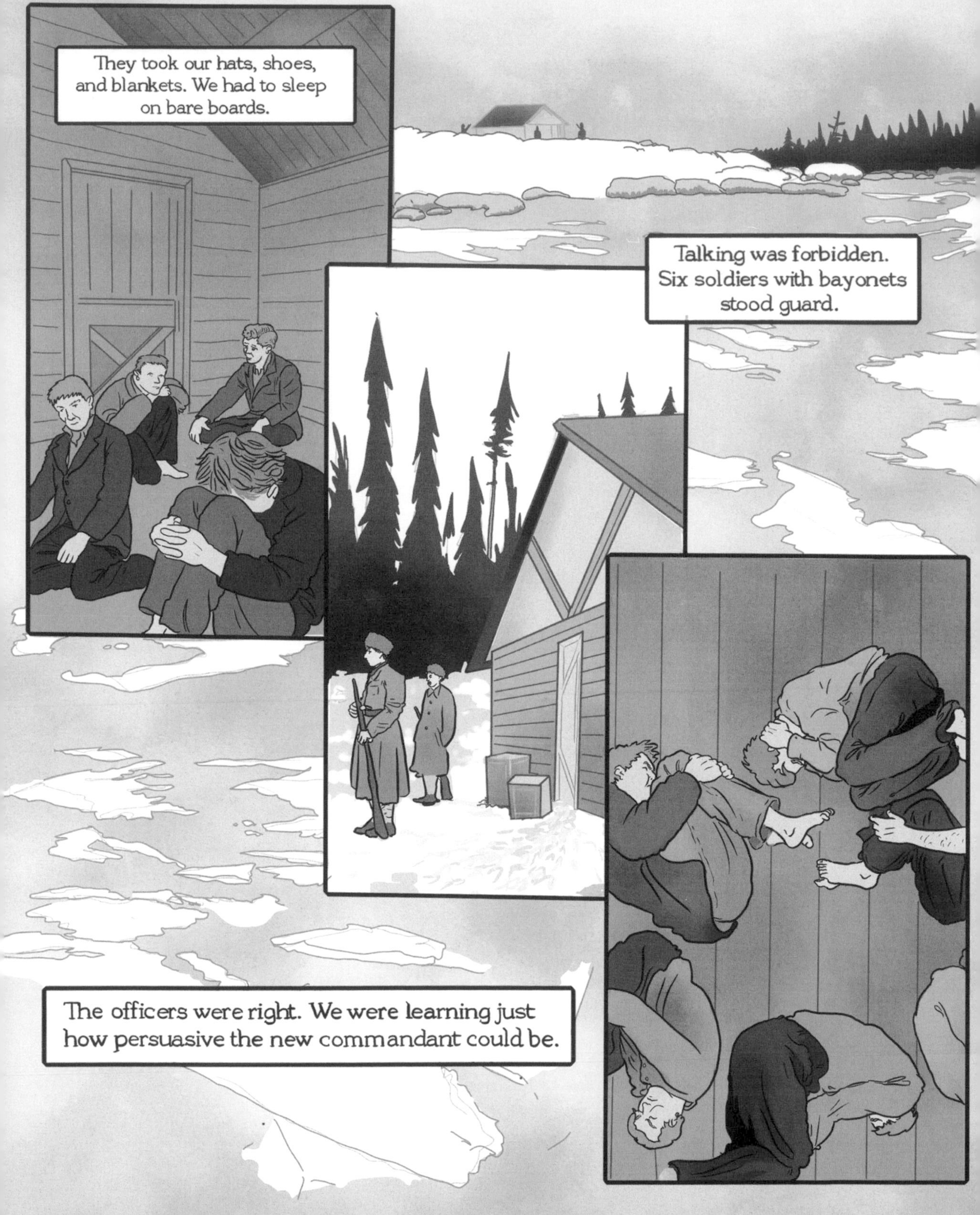
They took our hats, shoes, and blankets. We had to sleep on bare boards.
Talking was forbidden. Six soldiers with bayonets stood guard.
The officers were right. We were learning just how persuasive the new commandant could be.

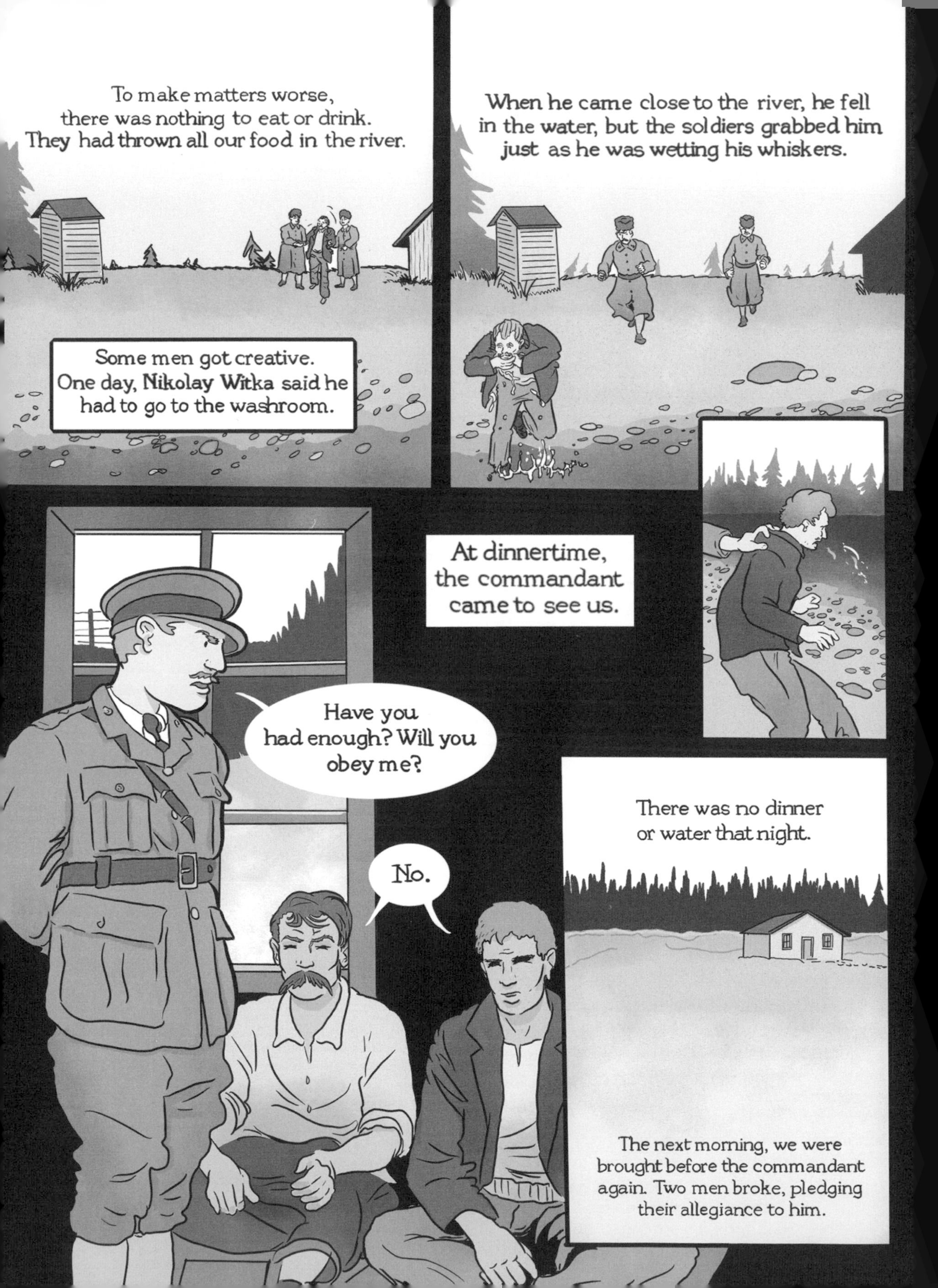

To make matters worse, there was nothing to eat or drink. They had thrown all our food in the river.
Some men got creative. One day, Nikolay Witka said he had to go to the washroom.
When he came close to the river, he fell in the water, but the soldiers grabbed him just as he was wetting his whiskers.
At dinnertime, the commandant came to see us.
Have you had enough? Will you obey me?
No.
There was no dinner or water that night.
The next morning, we were brought before the commandant again. Two men broke, pledging their allegiance to him.

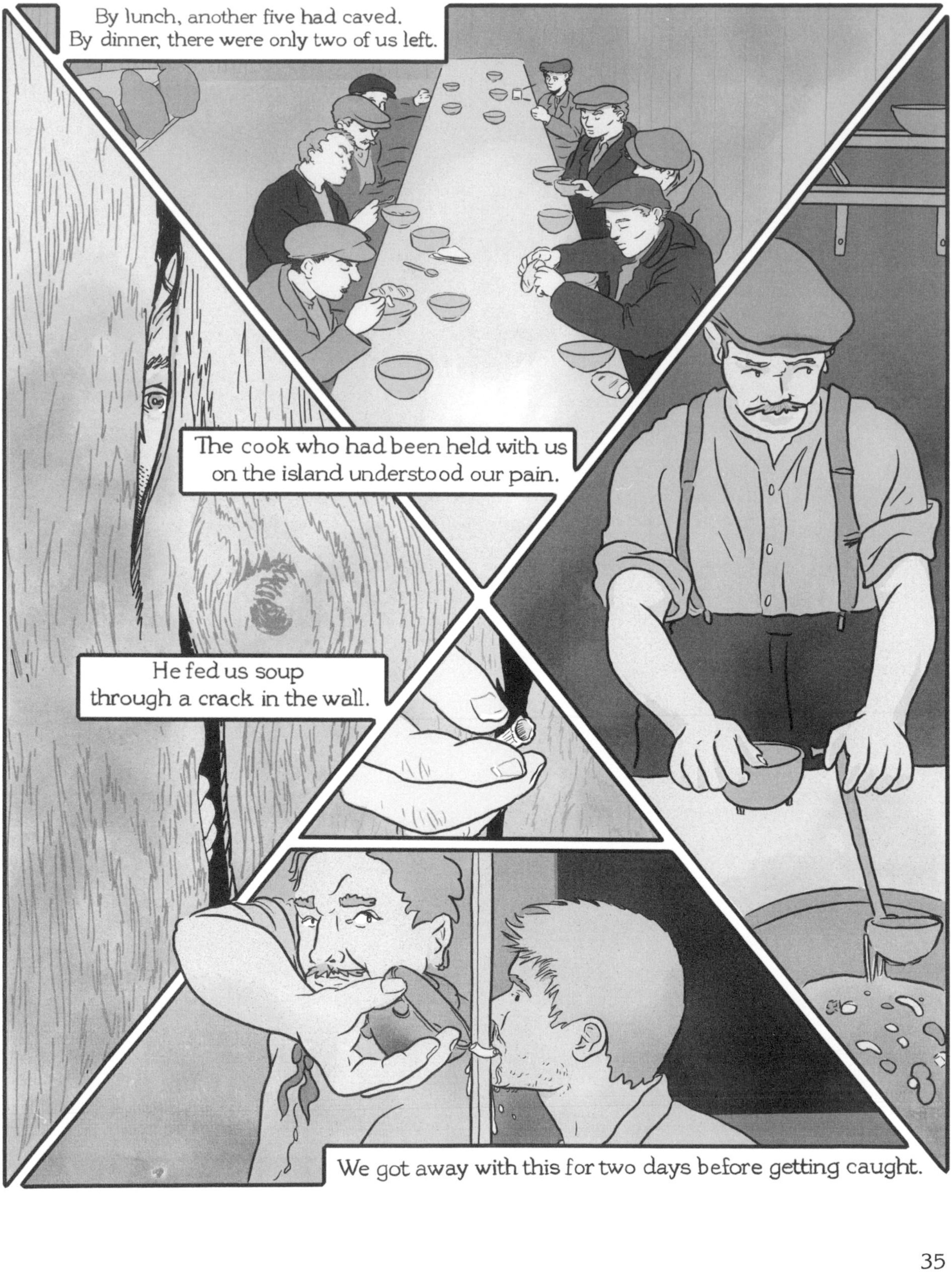
By lunch, another five had caved.
By dinner, there were only two of us left.
The cook who had been held with us on the island understood our pain.
He fed us soup through a crack in the wall.
We got away with this for two days before getting caught.

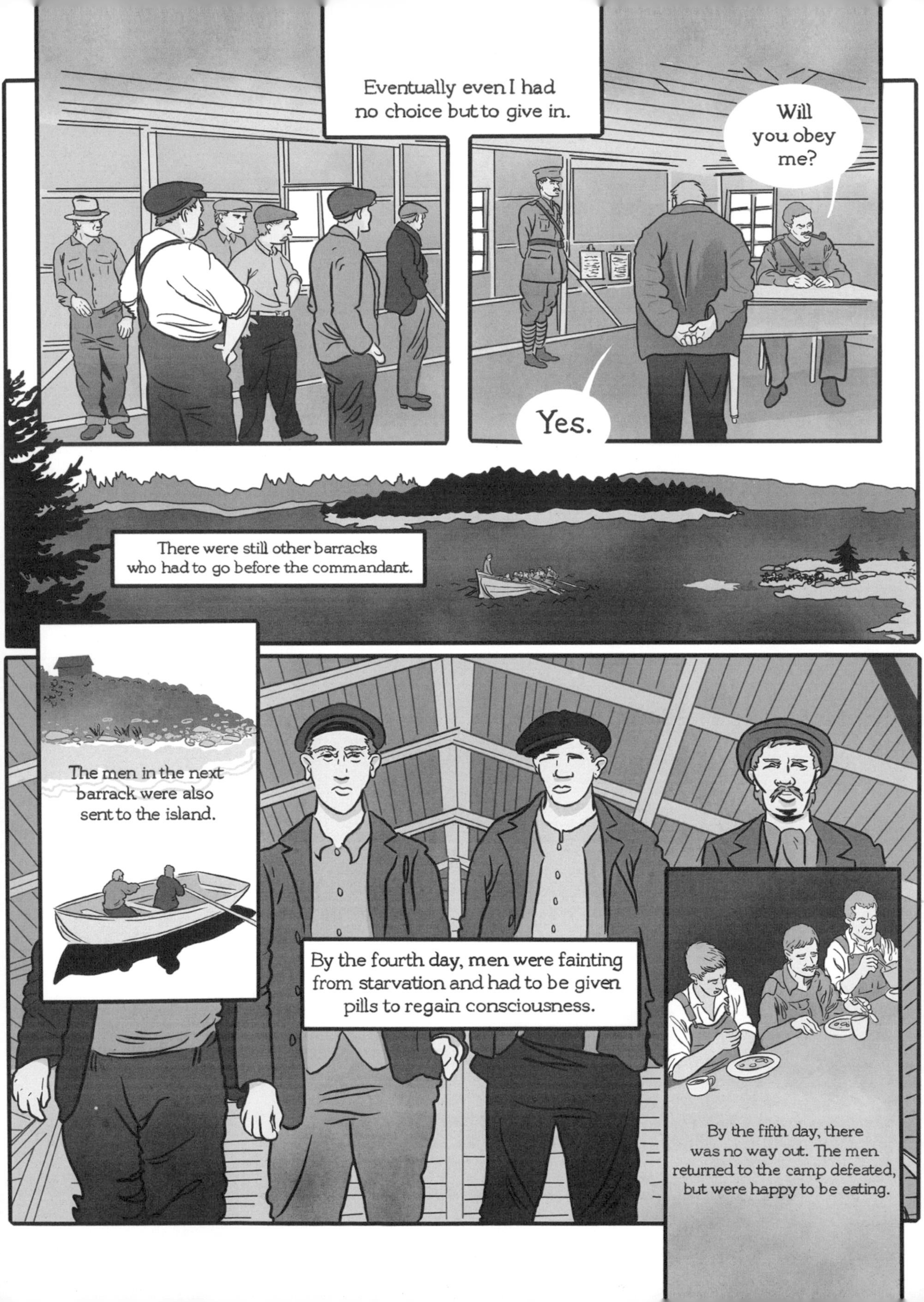
Eventually even I had no choice but to give in.
Will you obey me?
Yes.
There were still other barracks who had to go before the commandant.
The men in the next barrack were also sent to the island.
By the fourth day, men were fainting from starvation and had to be given pills to regain consciousness.
By the fifth day, there was no way out. The men returned to the camp defeated, but were happy to be eating.

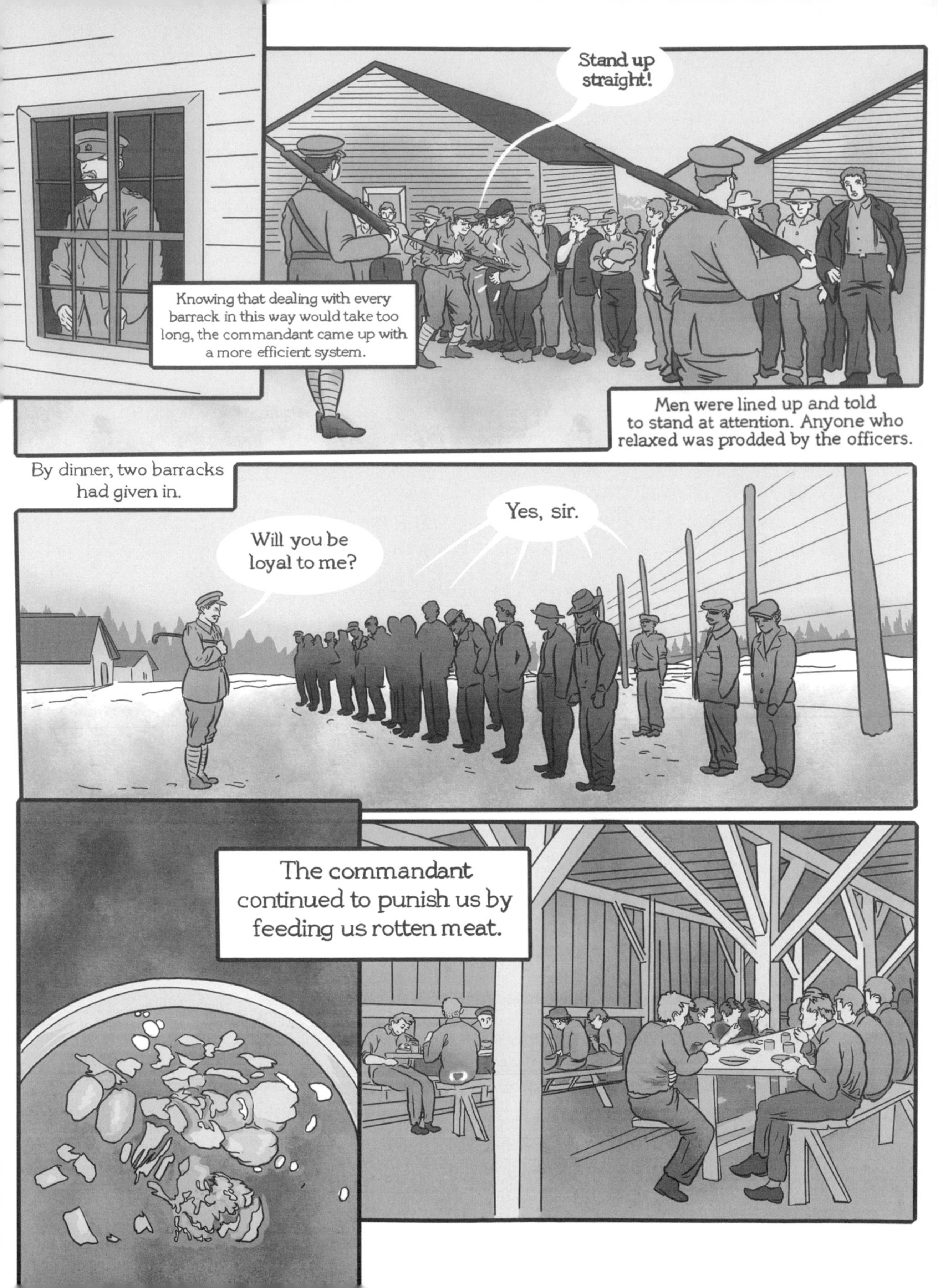
Stand up straight!
Knowing that dealing with every barrack in this way would take too long, the commandant came up with a more efficient system.
Men were lined up and told to stand at attention. Anyone who relaxed was prodded by the officers.
By dinner, two barracks had given in.
Will you be loyal to me?
Yes, sir.
The commandant continued to punish us by feeding us rotten meat.

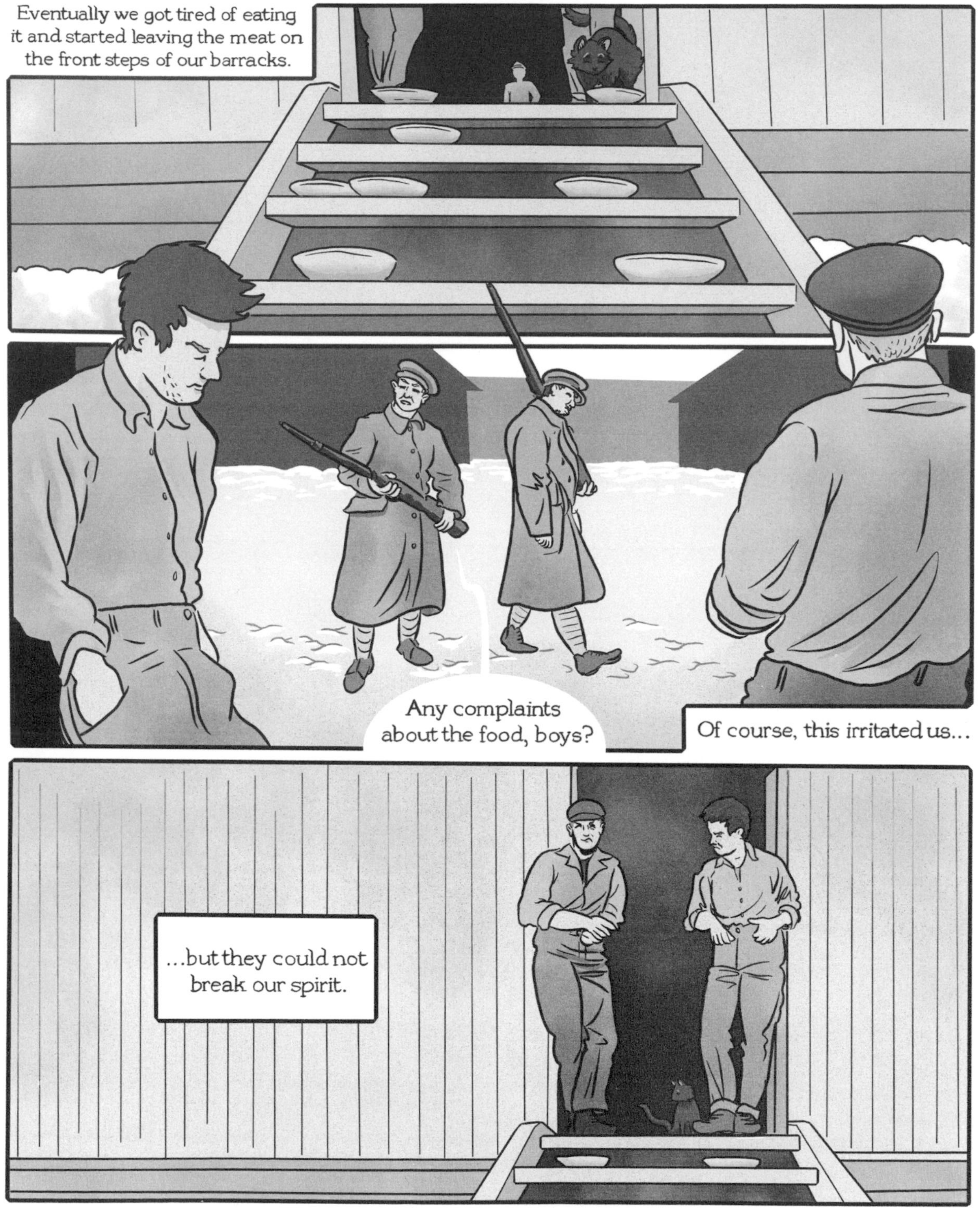
Eventually we got tired of eating it and started leaving the meat on the front steps of our barracks.
Any complaints about the food, boys?
Of course, this irritated us...
...but they could not break our spirit.

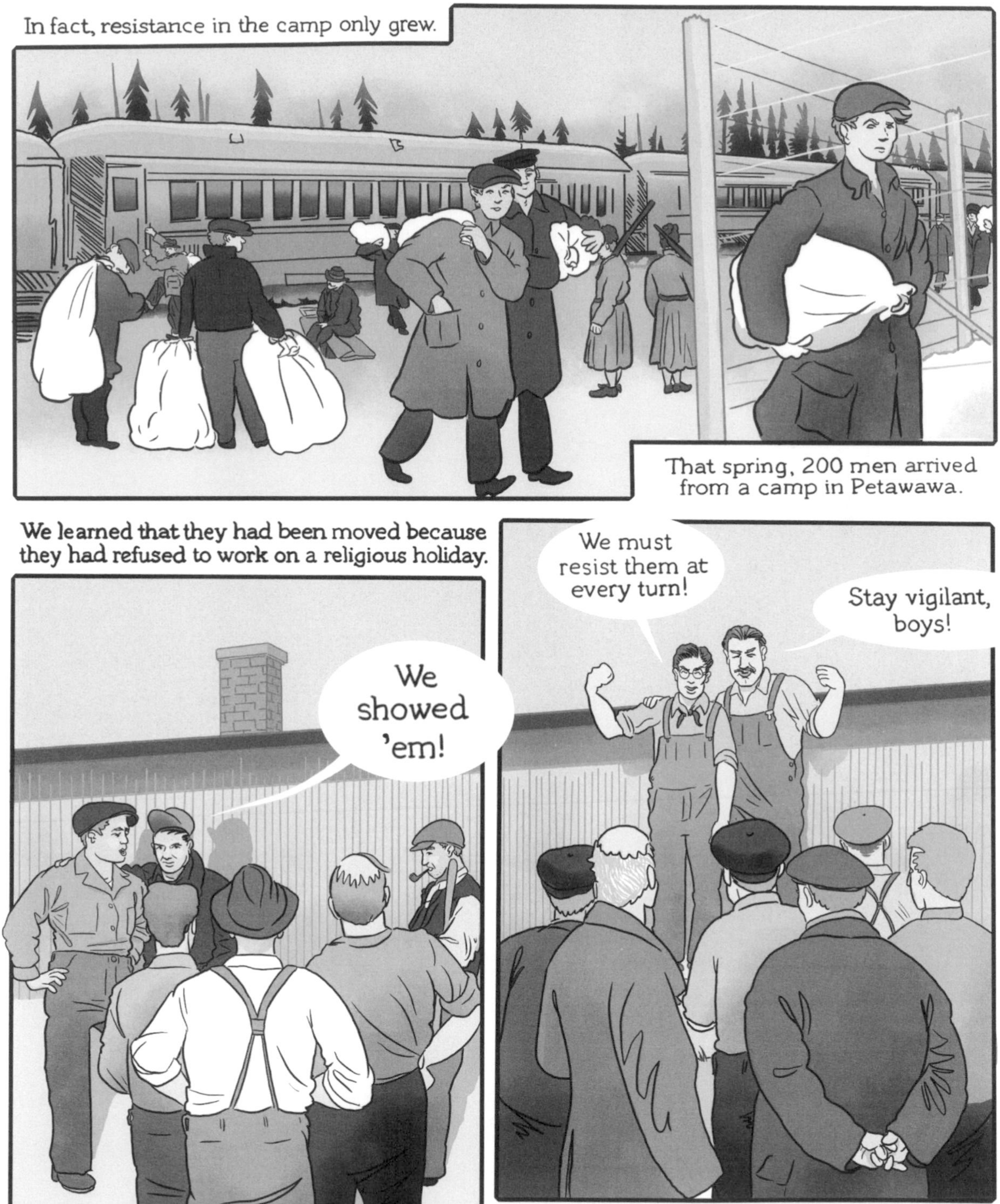
In fact, resistance in the camp only grew.
That spring, 200 men arrived from a camp in Petawawa.
We learned that they had been moved because they had refused to work on a religious holiday.
We showed 'em!
We must resist them at every turn!
Stay vigilant, boys!
The men from Petawawa were gifted orators. Their message spread quickly throughout the camp.

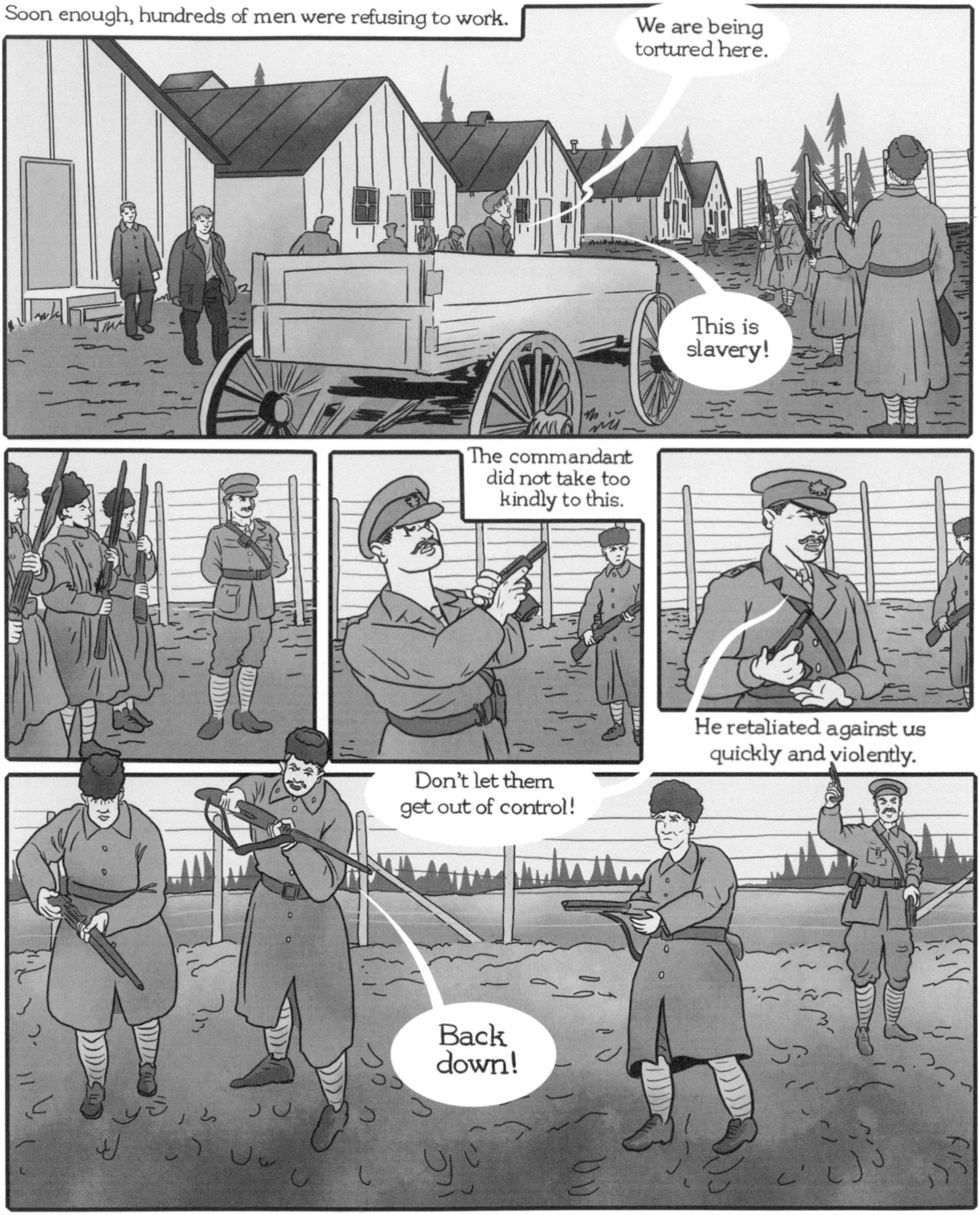
Soon enough, hundreds of men were refusing to work.
We are being tortured here.
This is slavery!
The commandant did not take too kindly to this.
He retaliated against us quickly and violently.
Don't let them get out of control!
Back down!

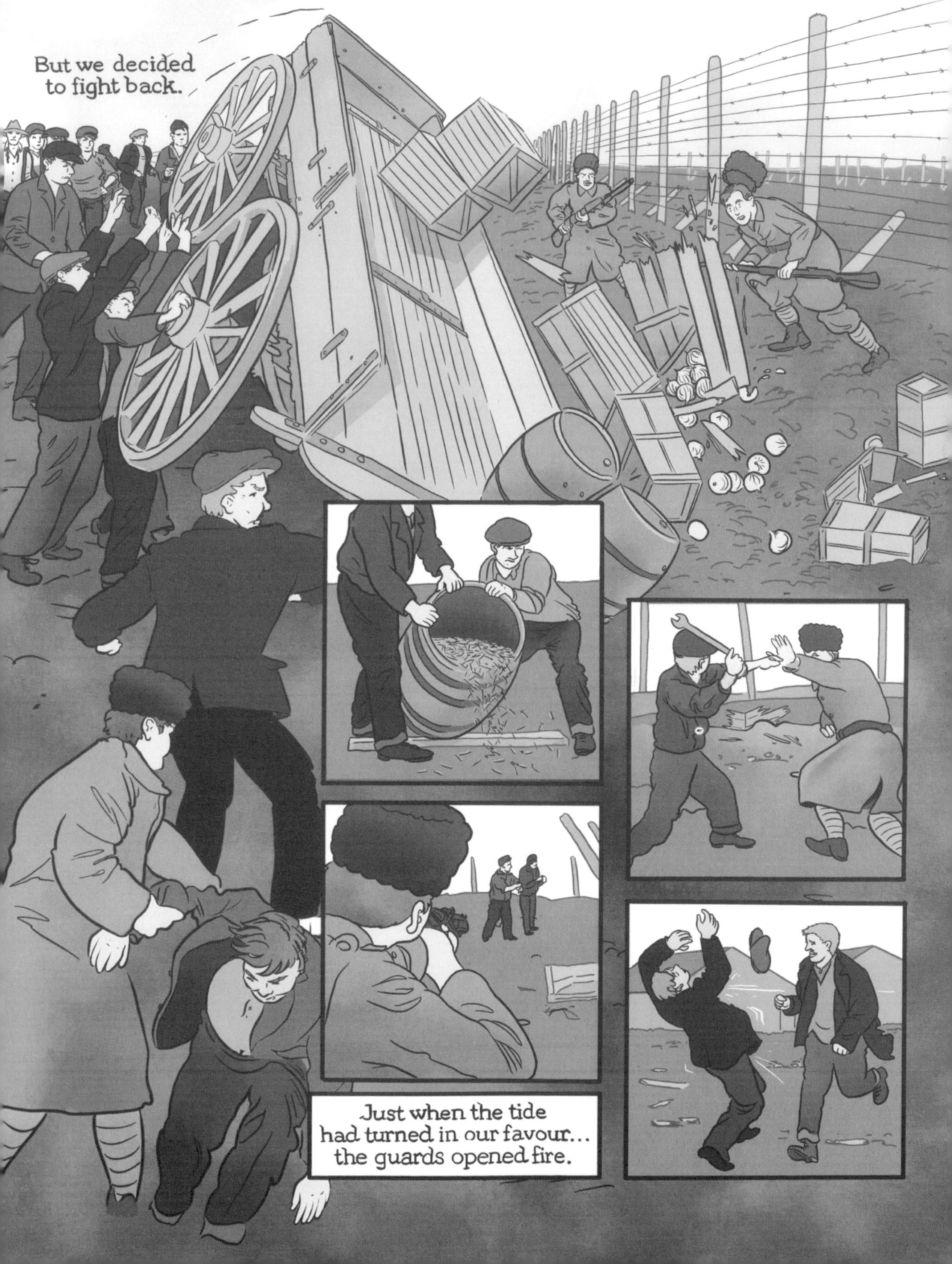
But we decided to fight back.
Just when the tide had turned in our favour... the guards opened fire.

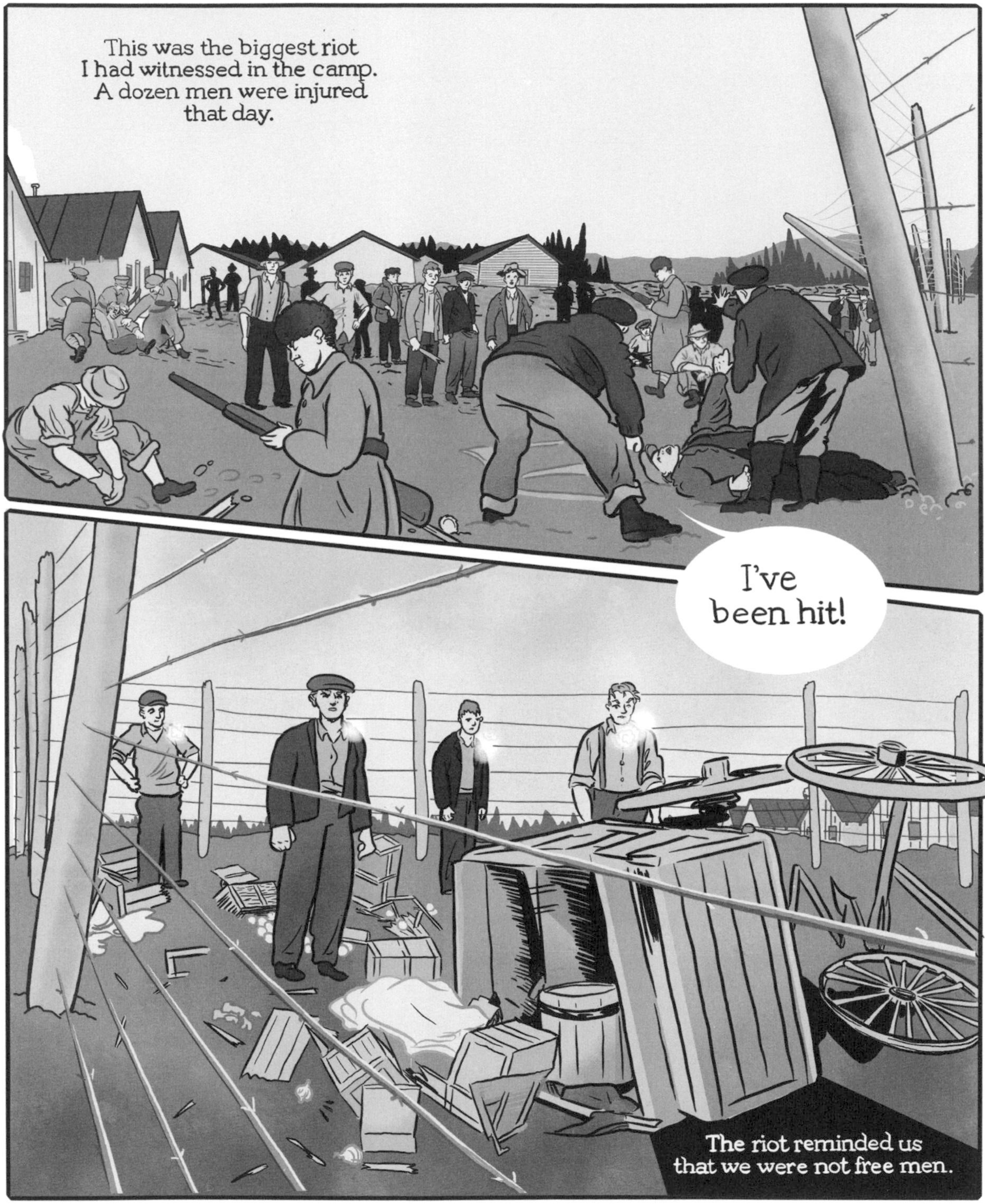
This was the biggest riot I had witnessed in the camp. A dozen men were injured that day.
I've been hit!
The riot reminded us that we were not free men.

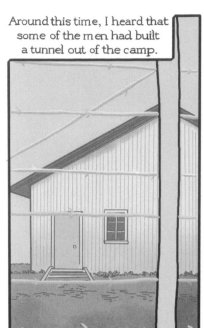

Around this time, I heard that some of the men had built a tunnel out of the camp.

Apparently it started in Bunkhouse #1 in the second-class yard...

...though how anyone even attempted such a thing under constant guard is a mystery.

The door was hidden under a small seaman's chest.

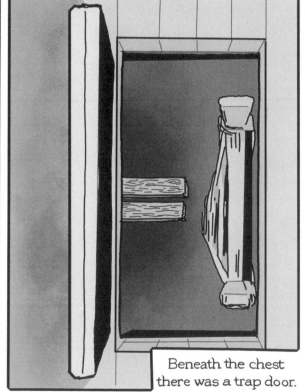

Beneath the chest there was a trap door.

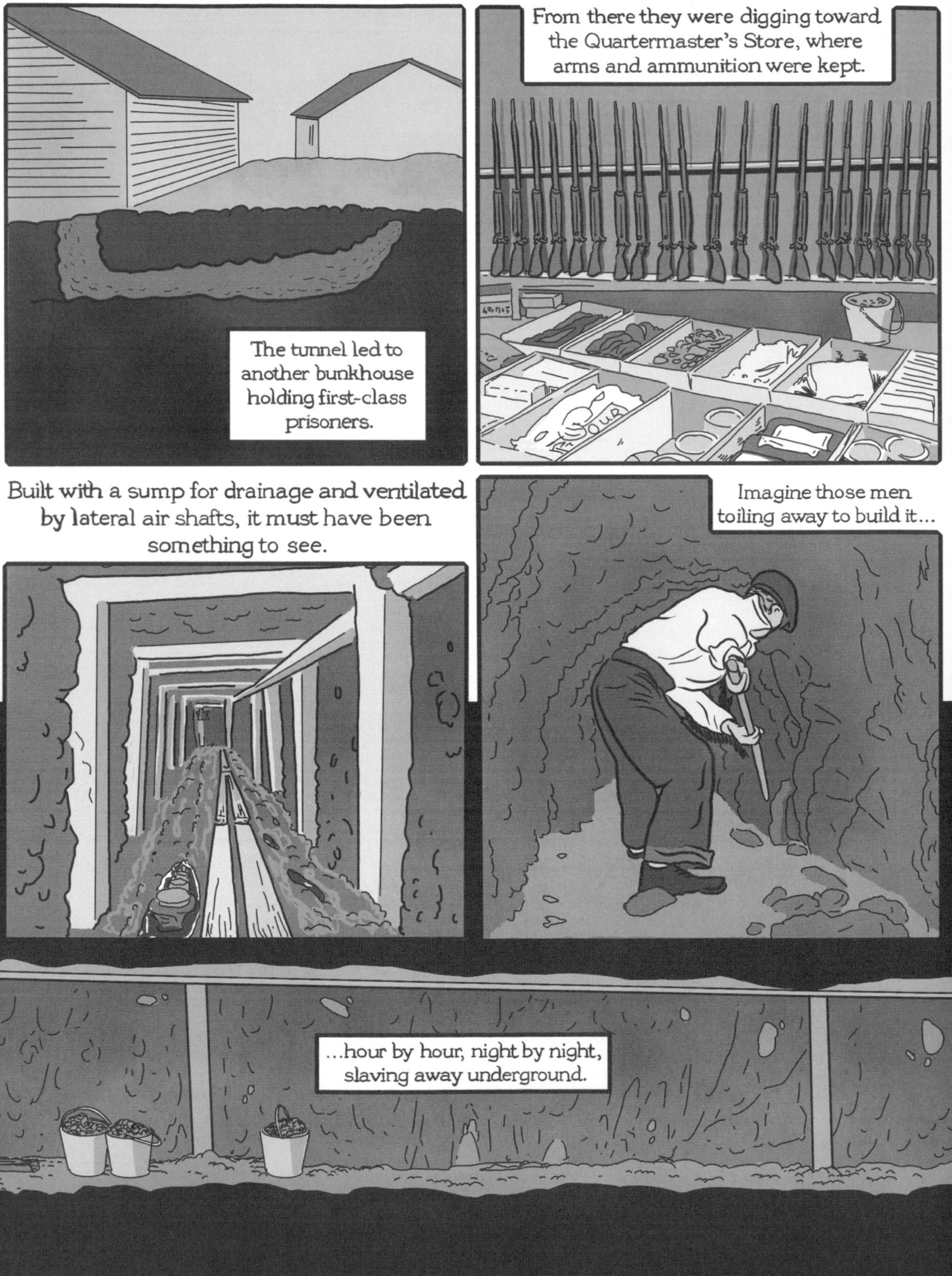
The tunnel led to another bunkhouse holding first-class prisoners.
From there they were digging toward the Quartermaster's Store, where arms and ammunition were kept.
Built with a sump for drainage and ventilated by lateral air shafts, it must have been something to see.
Imagine those men toiling away to build it...
...hour by hour, night by night, slaving away underground.

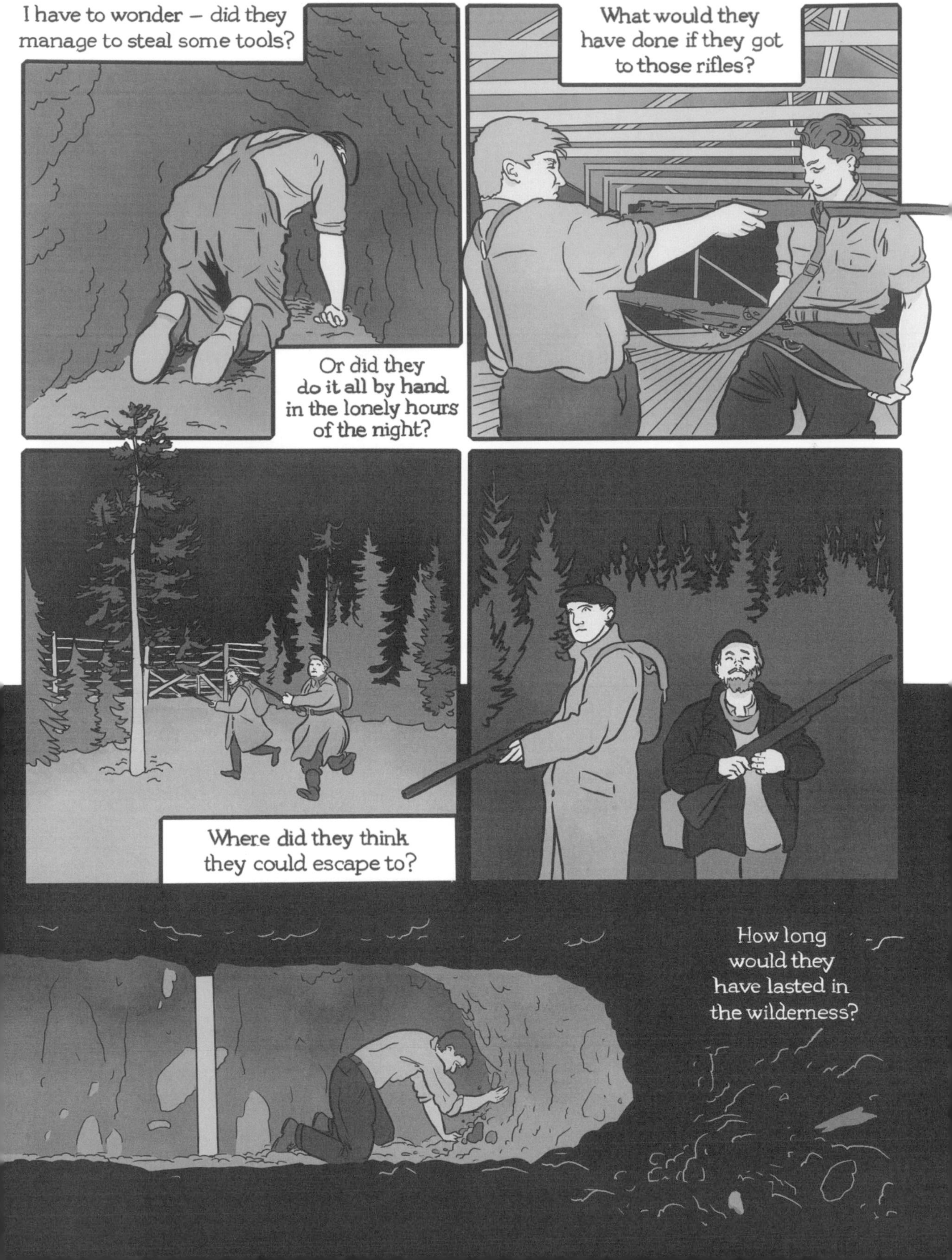
I have to wonder – did they manage to steal some tools?
Or did they do it all by hand in the lonely hours of the night?
What would they have done if they got to those rifles?
Where did they think they could escape to?
How long would they have lasted in the wilderness?

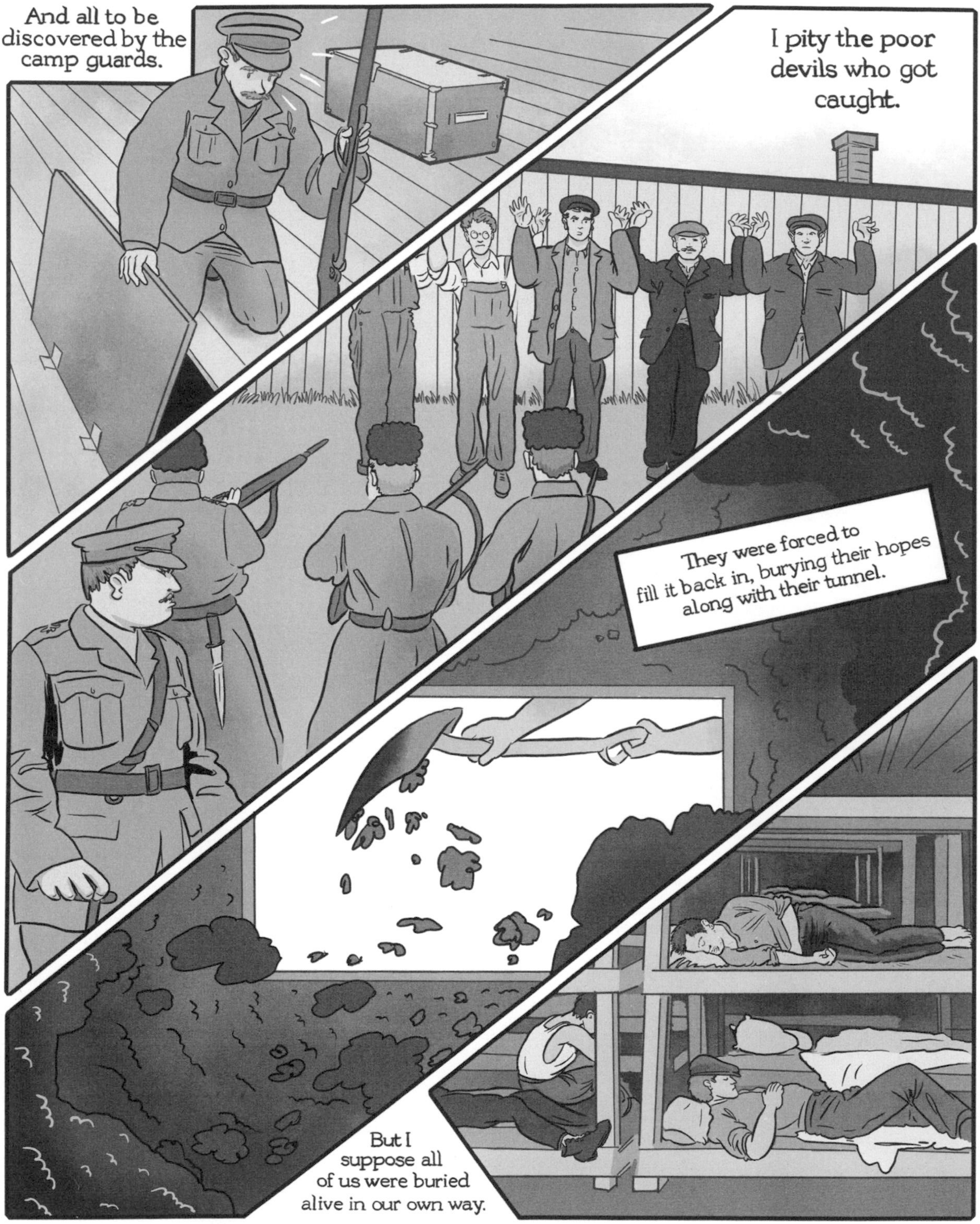

And all to be discovered by the camp guards.
I pity the poor devils who got caught.
They were forced to fill it back in, burying their hopes along with their tunnel.
But I suppose all of us were buried alive in our own way.

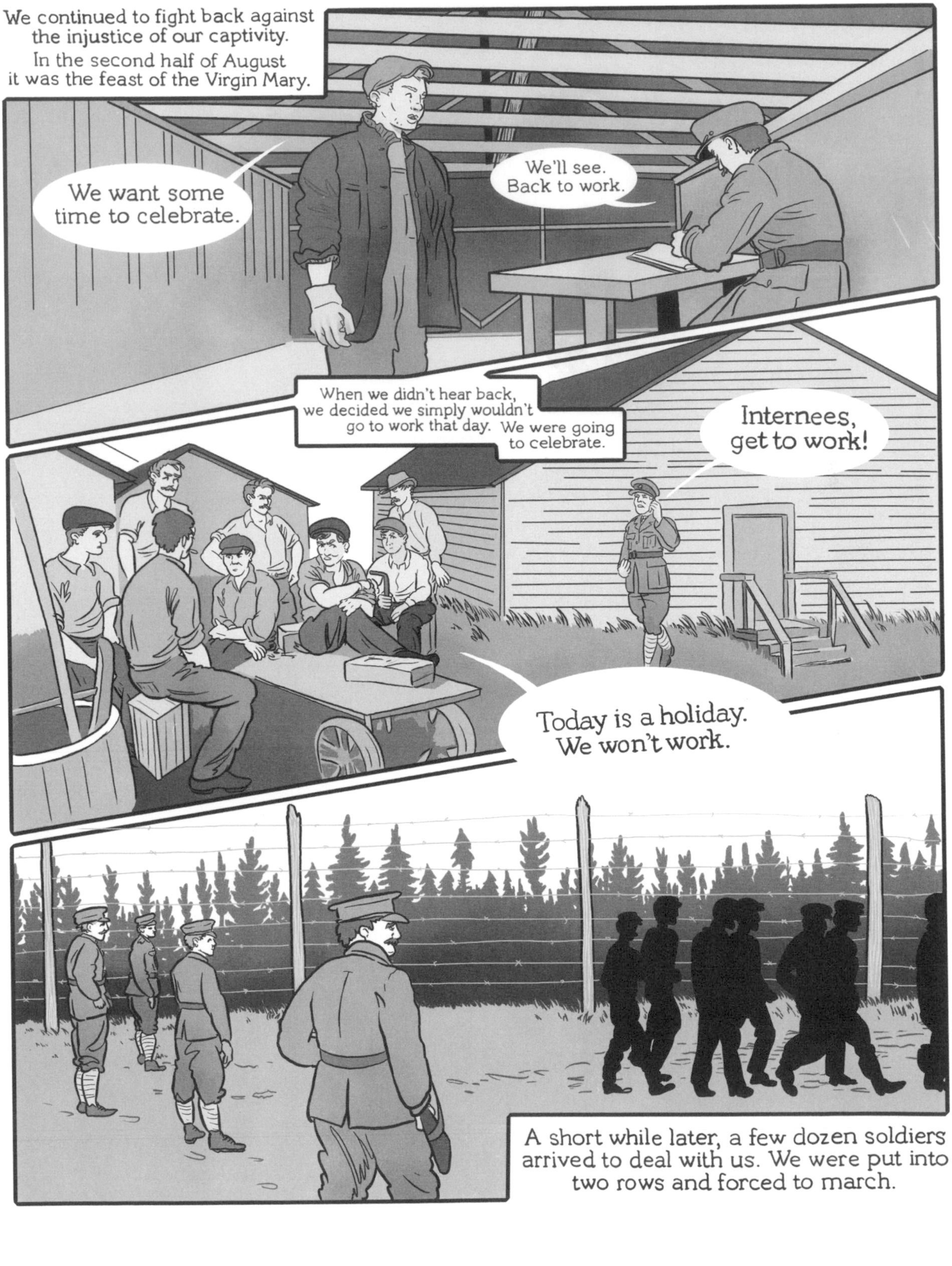

We continued to fight back against the injustice of our captivity.
In the second half of August it was the feast of the Virgin Mary.
We want some time to celebrate.
We'll see. Back to work.
When we didn't hear back, we decided we simply wouldn't go to work that day. We were going to celebrate.
Internees, get to work!
Today is a holiday. We won't work.
A short while later, a few dozen soldiers arrived to deal with us. We were put into two rows and forced to march.

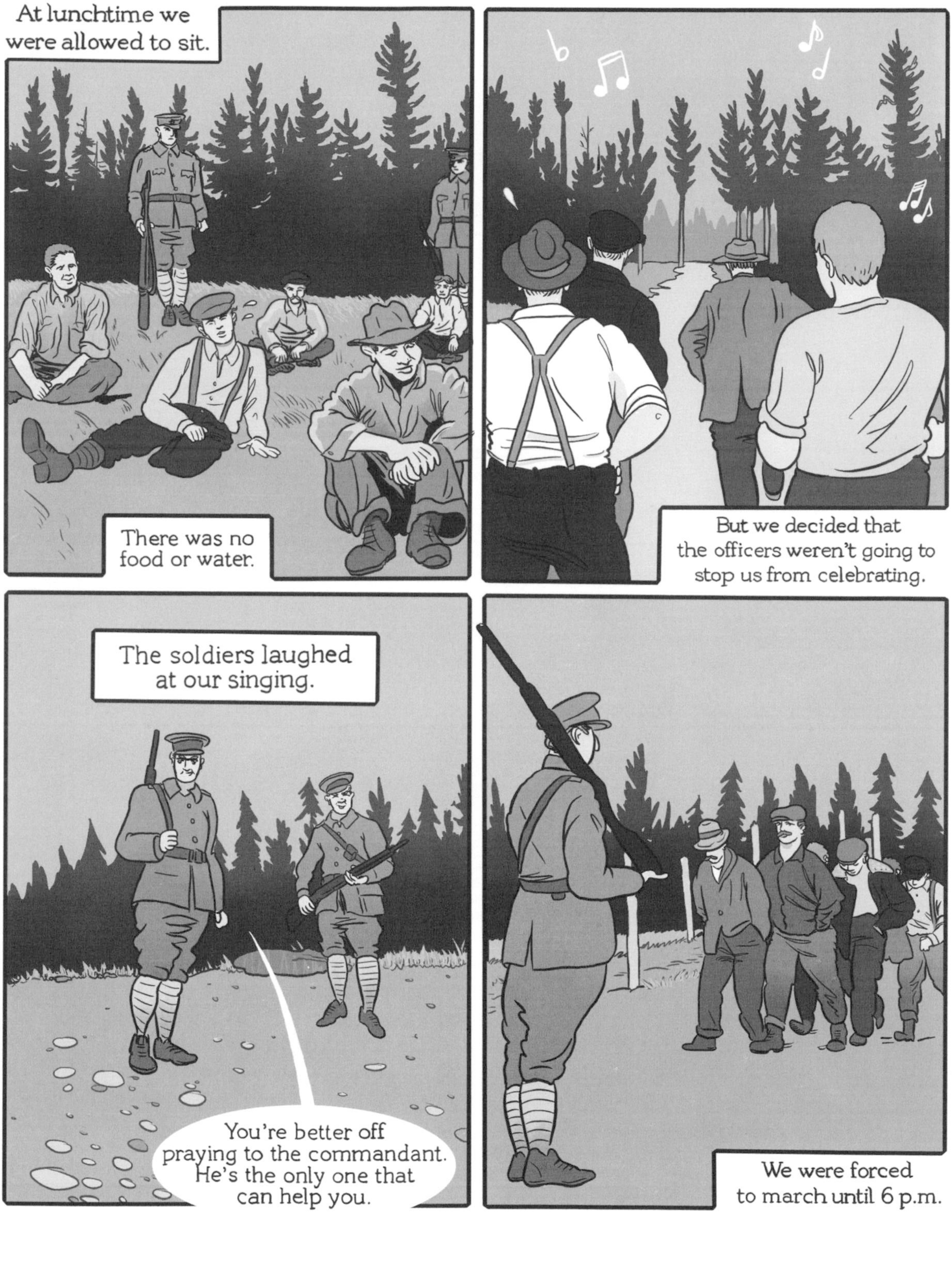
At lunchtime we were allowed to sit.
There was no food or water.
But we decided that the officers weren't going to stop us from celebrating.
The soldiers laughed at our singing.
You're better off praying to the commandant. He's the only one that can help you.
We were forced to march until 6 p.m.

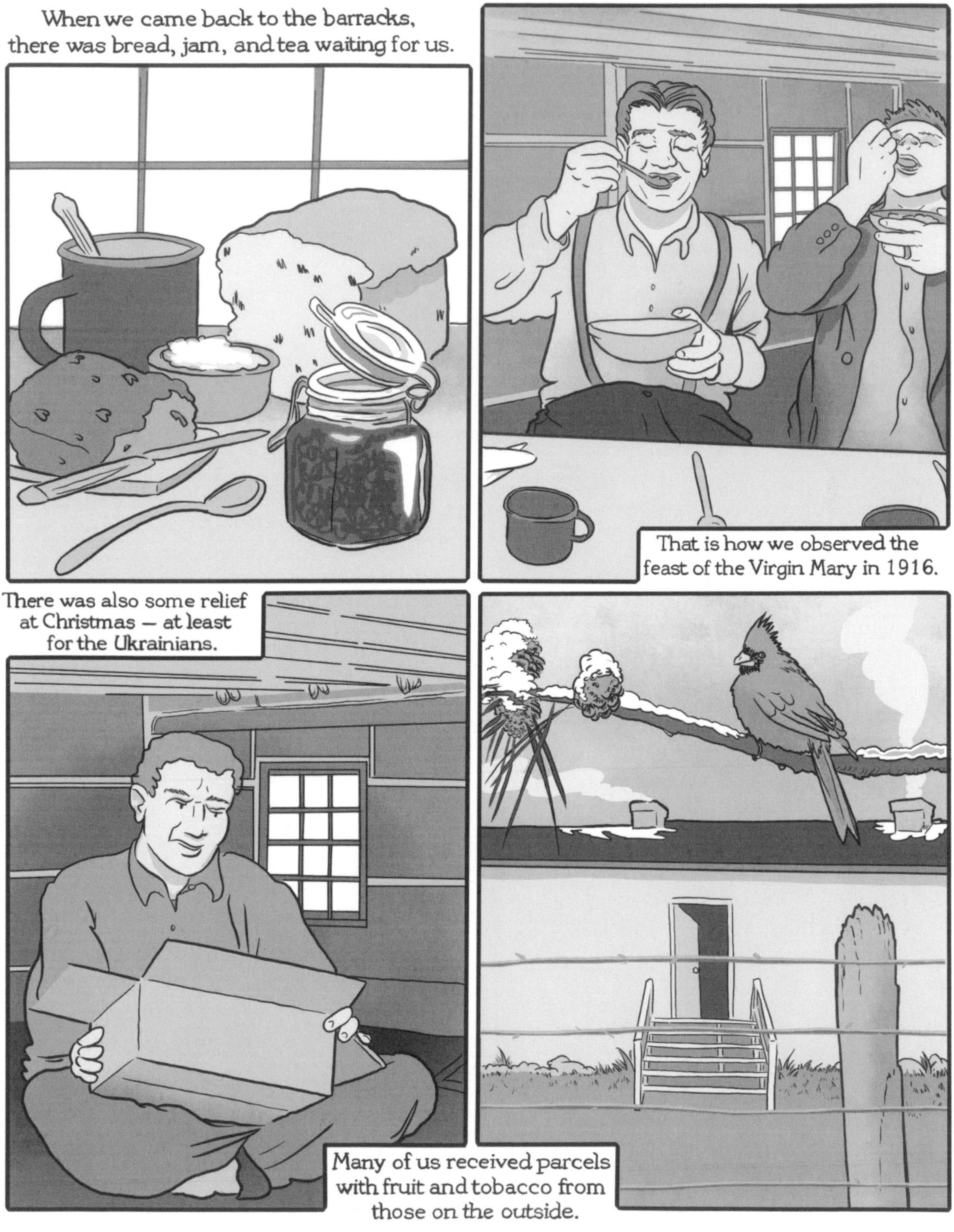
When we came back to the barracks, there was bread, jam, and tea waiting for us.
That is how we observed the feast of the Virgin Mary in 1916.
There was also some relief at Christmas — at least for the Ukrainians.
Many of us received parcels with fruit and tobacco from those on the outside.

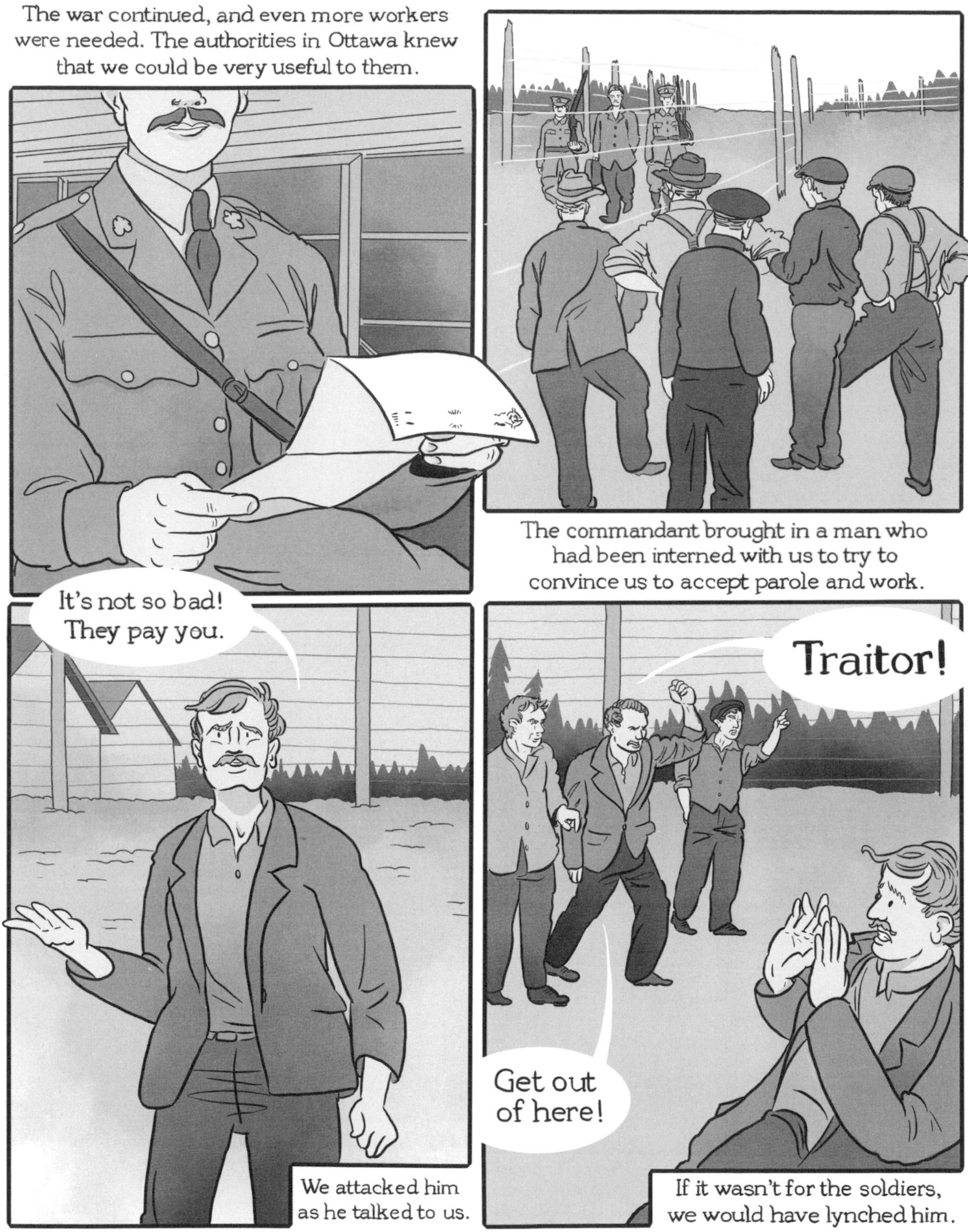
The war continued, and even more workers were needed. The authorities in Ottawa knew that we could be very useful to them.
The commandant brought in a man who had been interned with us to try to convince us to accept parole and work.
It's not so bad! They pay you.
We attacked him as he talked to us.
Traitor!
Get out of here!
If it wasn't for the soldiers, we would have lynched him.

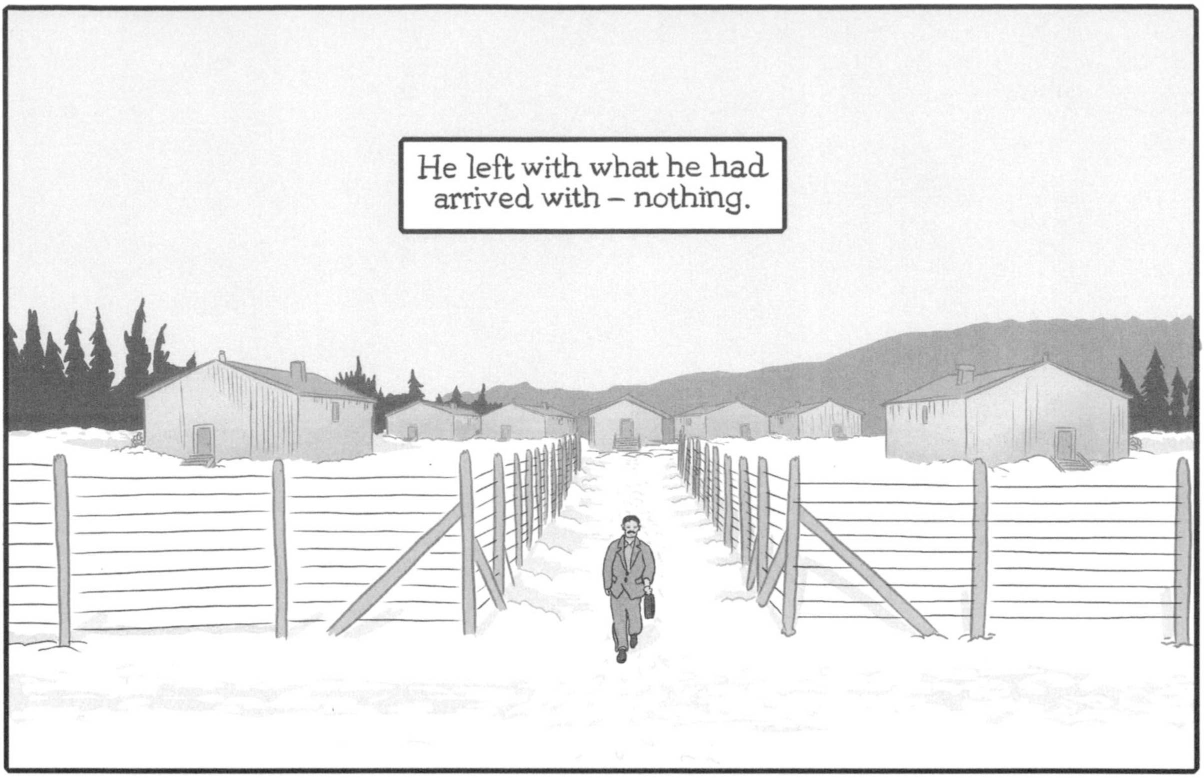
He left with what he had arrived with – nothing.

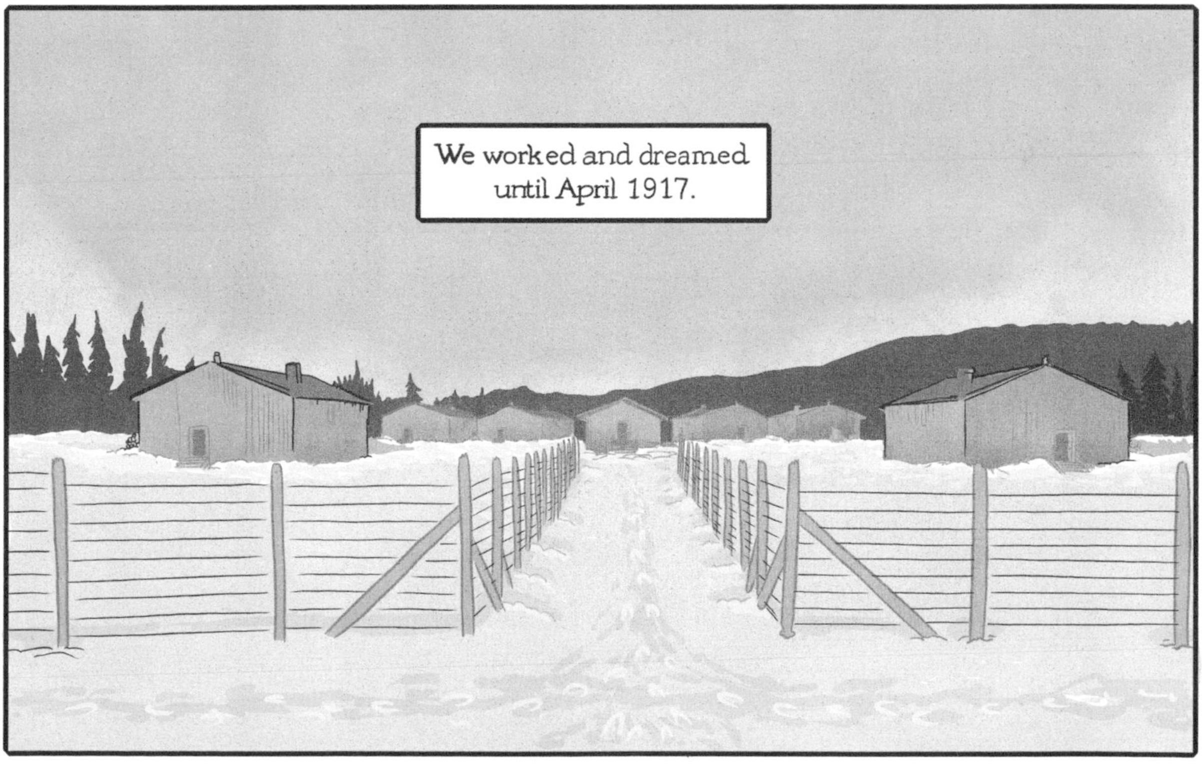
We worked and dreamed until April 1917.

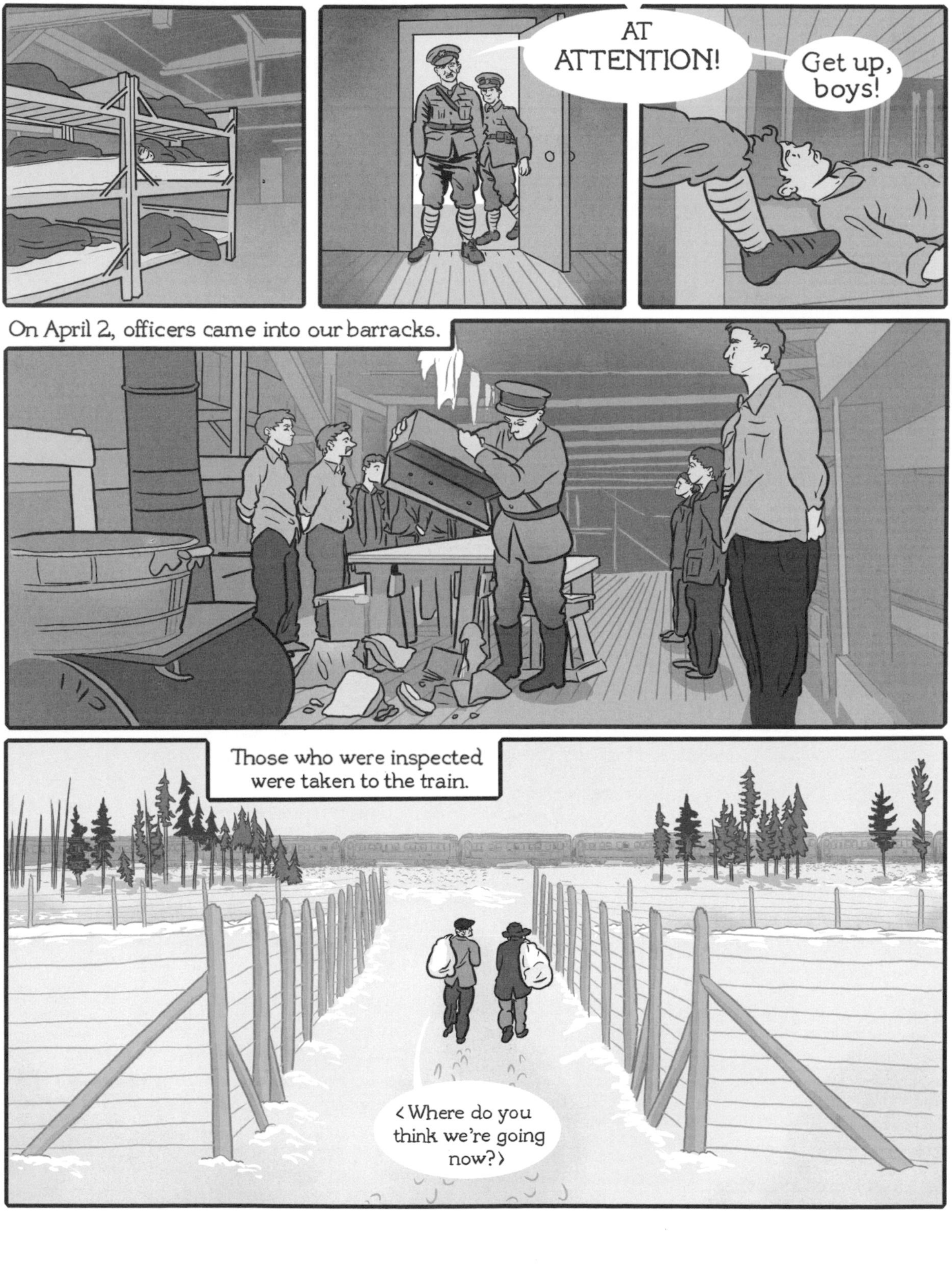
AT ATTENTION!
Get up, boys!
On April 2, officers came into our barracks.
Those who were inspected were taken to the train.
<Where do you think we're going now?>

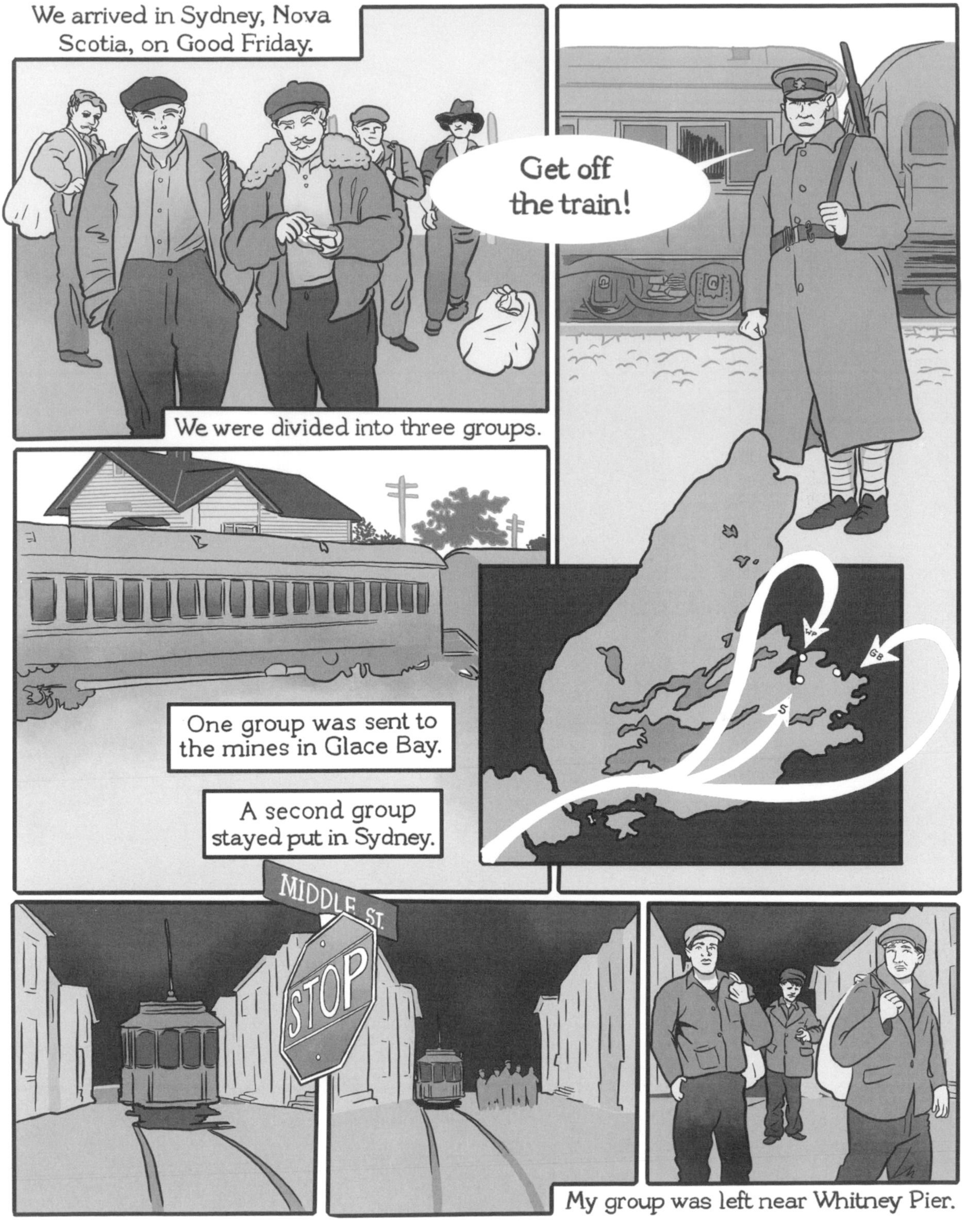
We arrived in Sydney, Nova Scotia, on Good Friday.
Get off the train!
We were divided into three groups.
WP
GB
S
One group was sent to the mines in Glace Bay.
A second group stayed put in Sydney.
MIDDLE ST.
STOP
My group was left near Whitney Pier.

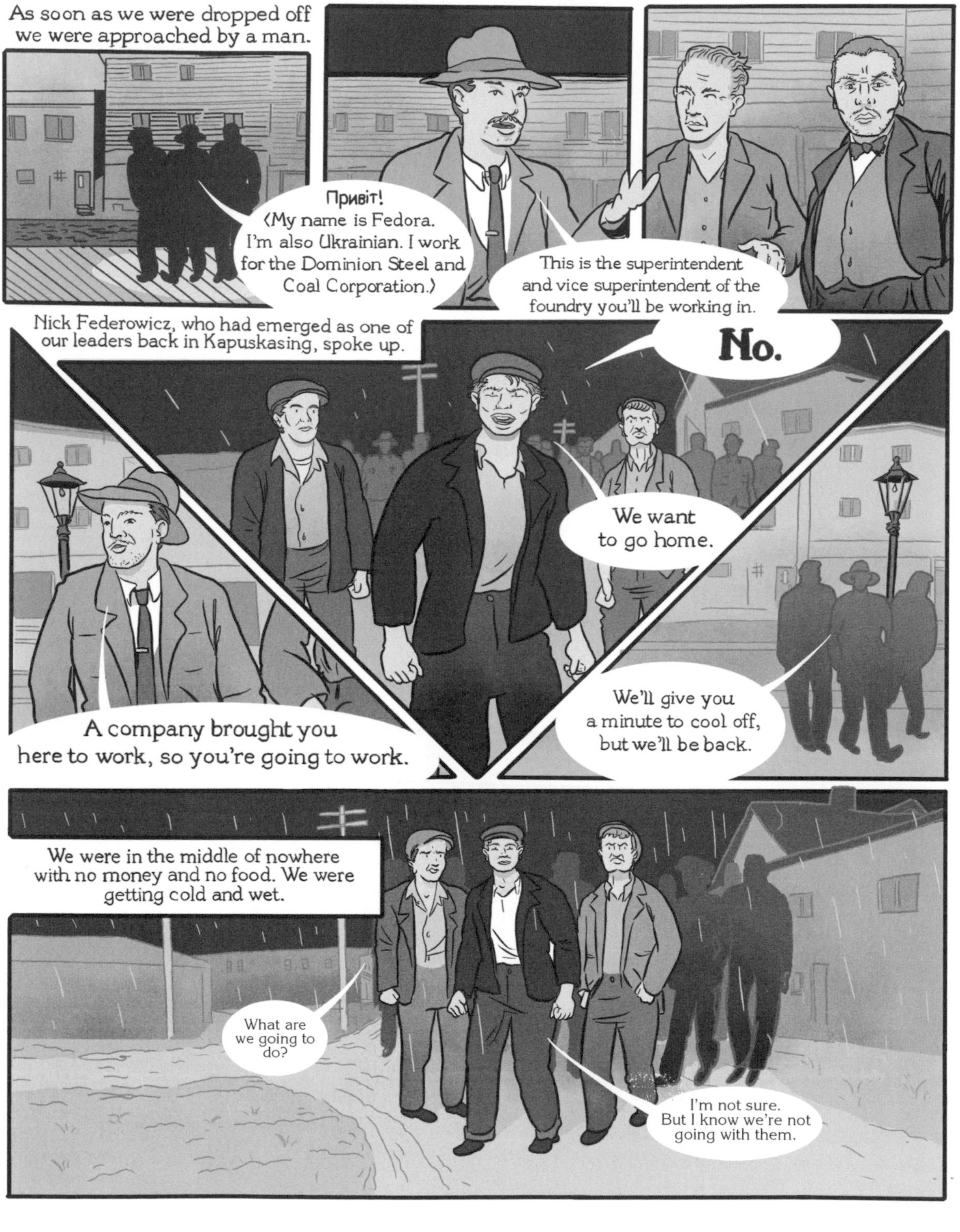

As soon as we were dropped off we were approached by a man.
Привіт! (My name is Fedora. I'm also Ukrainian. I work for the Dominion Steel and Coal Corporation.)
This is the superintendent and vice superintendent of the foundry you'll be working in.
Nick Federowicz, who had emerged as one of our leaders back in Kapuskasing, spoke up.
No.
We want to go home.
A company brought you here to work, so you're going to work.
We'll give you a minute to cool off, but we'll be back.
We were in the middle of nowhere with no money and no food. We were getting cold and wet.
What are we going to do?
I'm not sure. But I know we're not going with them.

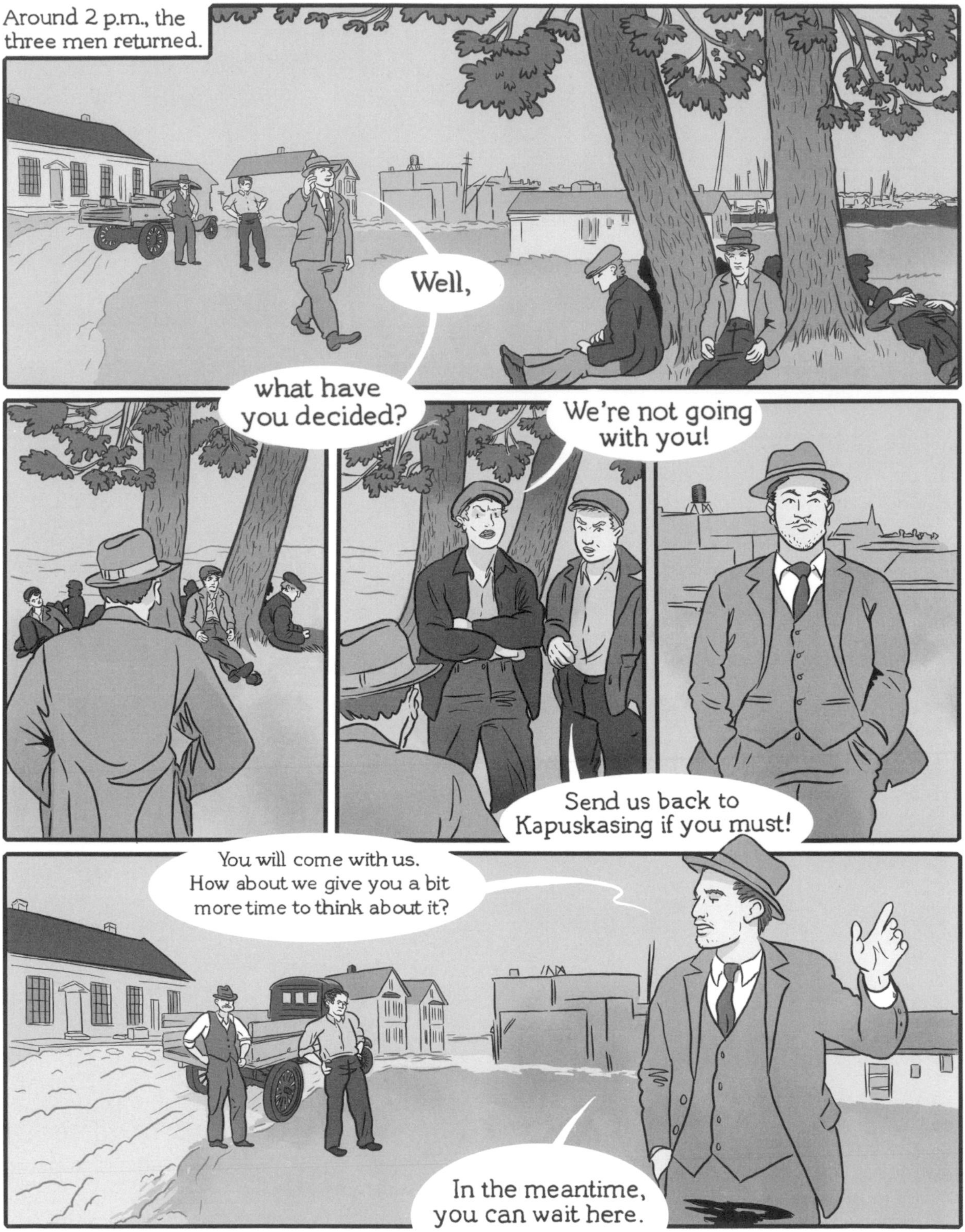
Around 2 p.m., the three men returned.
Well,
what have you decided?
We're not going with you!
Send us back to Kapuskasing if you must!
You will come with us. How about we give you a bit more time to think about it?
In the meantime, you can wait here.

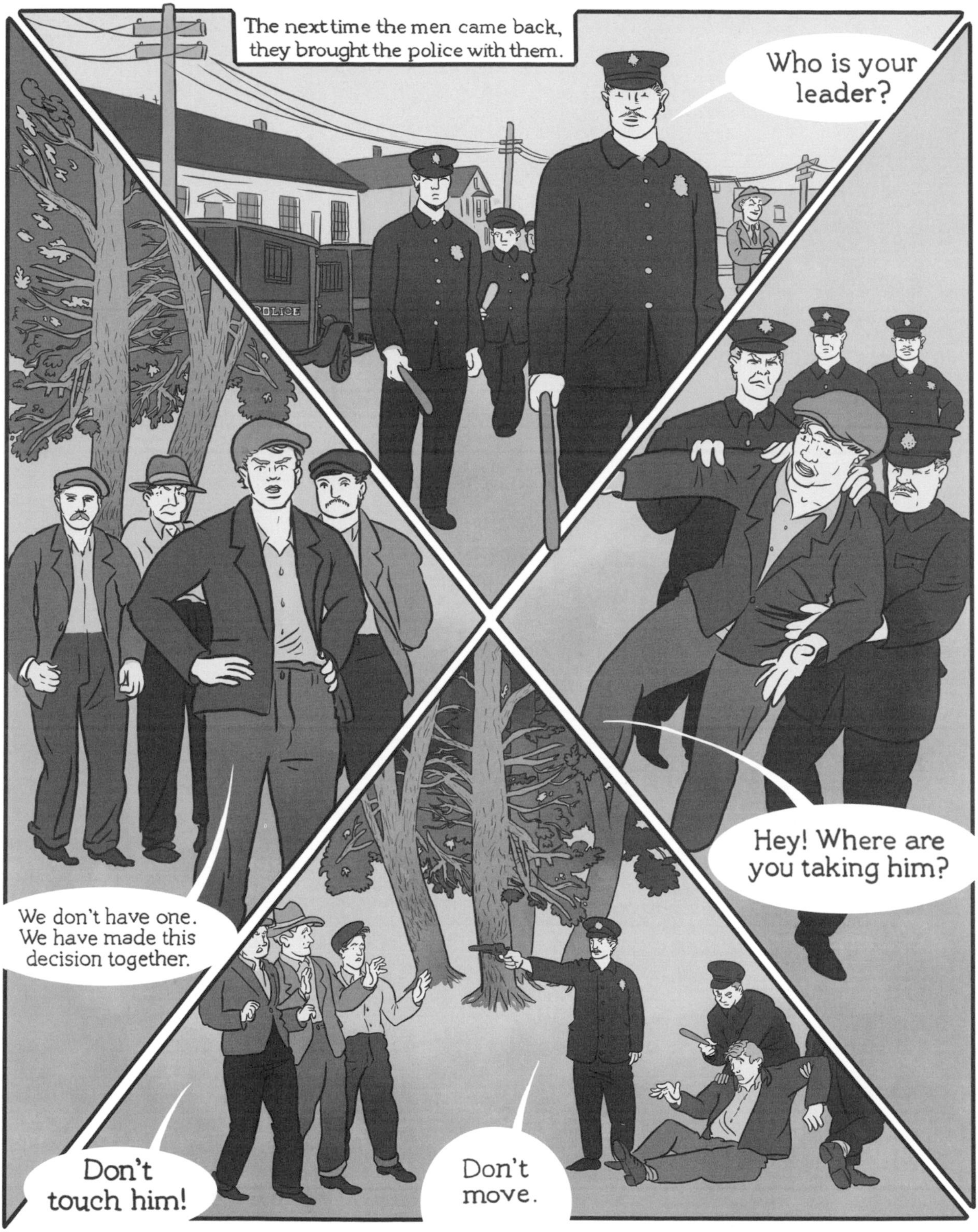
The next time the men came back, they brought the police with them.
Who is your leader?
POLICE
We don't have one. We have made this decision together.
Hey! Where are you taking him?
Don't touch him!
Don't move.

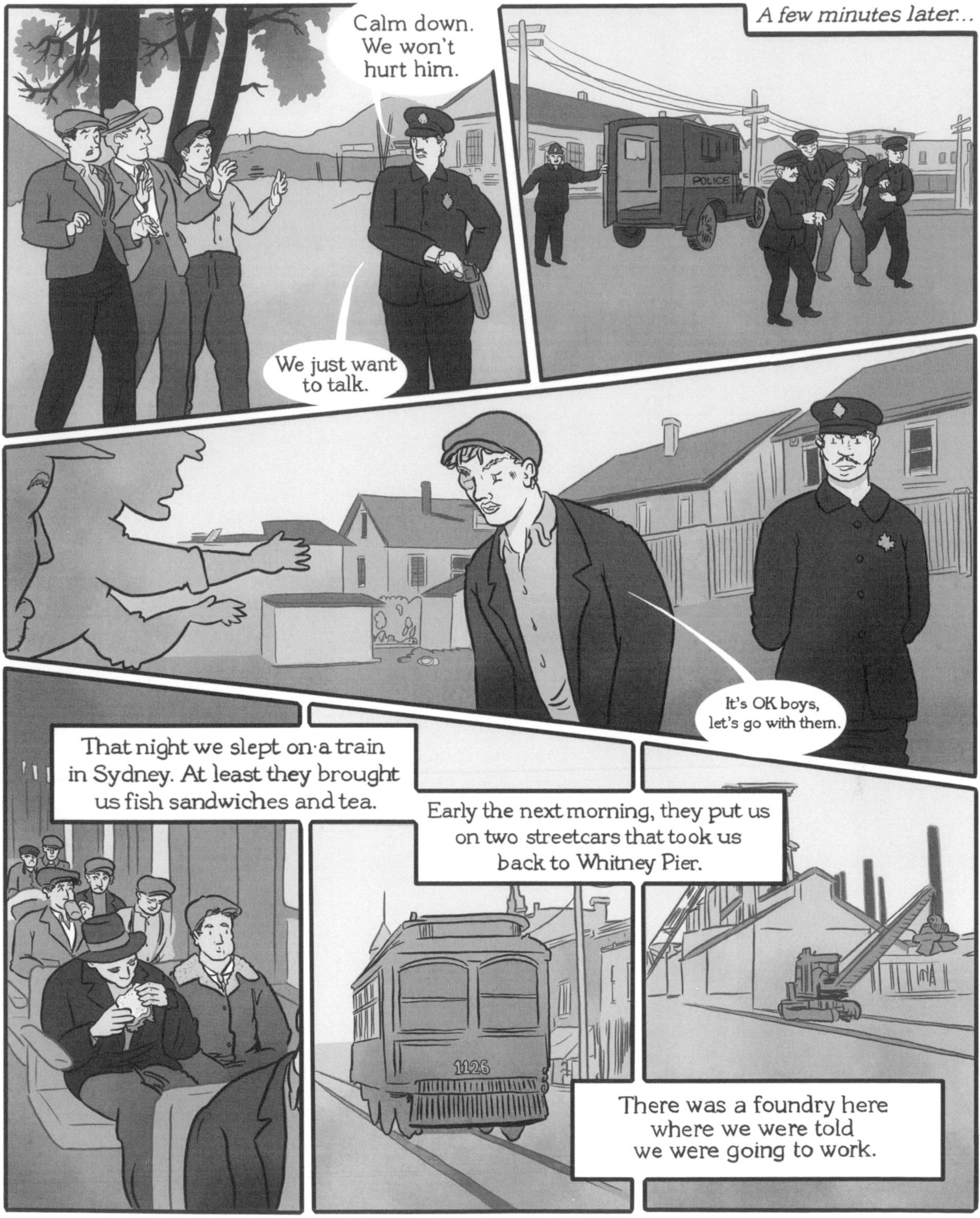
Calm down. We won't hurt him.
We just want to talk.
A few minutes later...
POLICE
It's OK boys, let's go with them.
That night we slept on a train in Sydney. At least they brought us fish sandwiches and tea.
Early the next morning, they put us on two streetcars that took us back to Whitney Pier.
1126
There was a foundry here where we were told we were going to work.

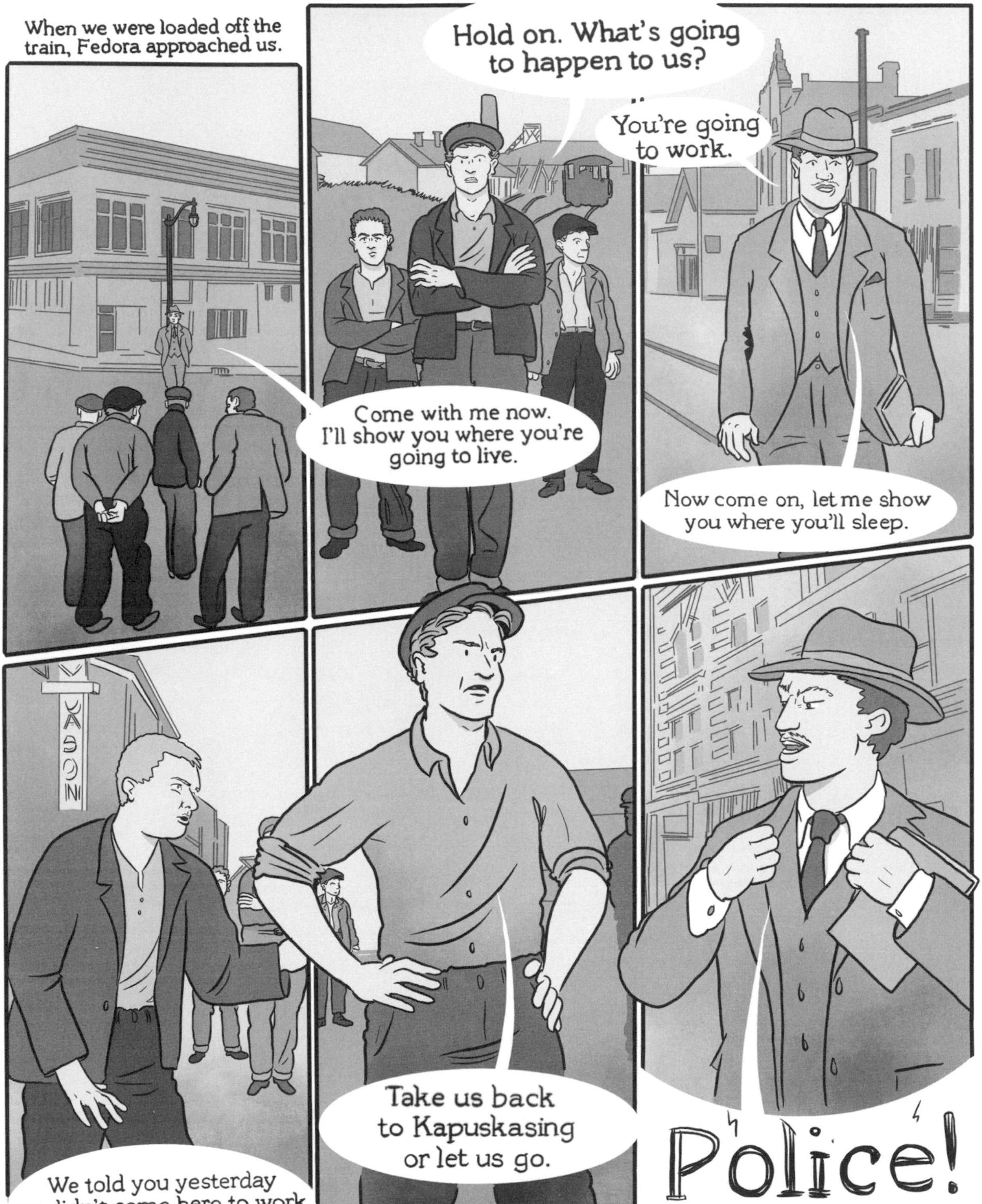

When we were loaded off the train, Fedora approached us.
Come with me now. I'll show you where you're going to live.
Hold on. What's going to happen to us?
You're going to work.
Now come on, let me show you where you'll sleep.
We told you yesterday we didn't come here to work.
Take us back to Kapuskasing or let us go.
Police!

Like wild animals, they fell upon us and beat us with clubs. Many men fell from their blows.

Soon enough, the police had herded us together.

Enough!

You will work!

Once again, it seemed like we had no choice.

I was put in an old wooden house with nine other Ukrainians and Poles. To celebrate Easter, we decided to dye some eggs together.

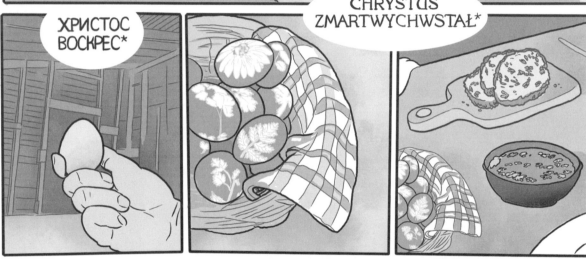

ХРИСТОС ВОСКРЕС*

CHRYSTUS ZMARTWYCHWSTAŁ*

It was a bloody Easter, but it ended well.

*Christ has risen.

60

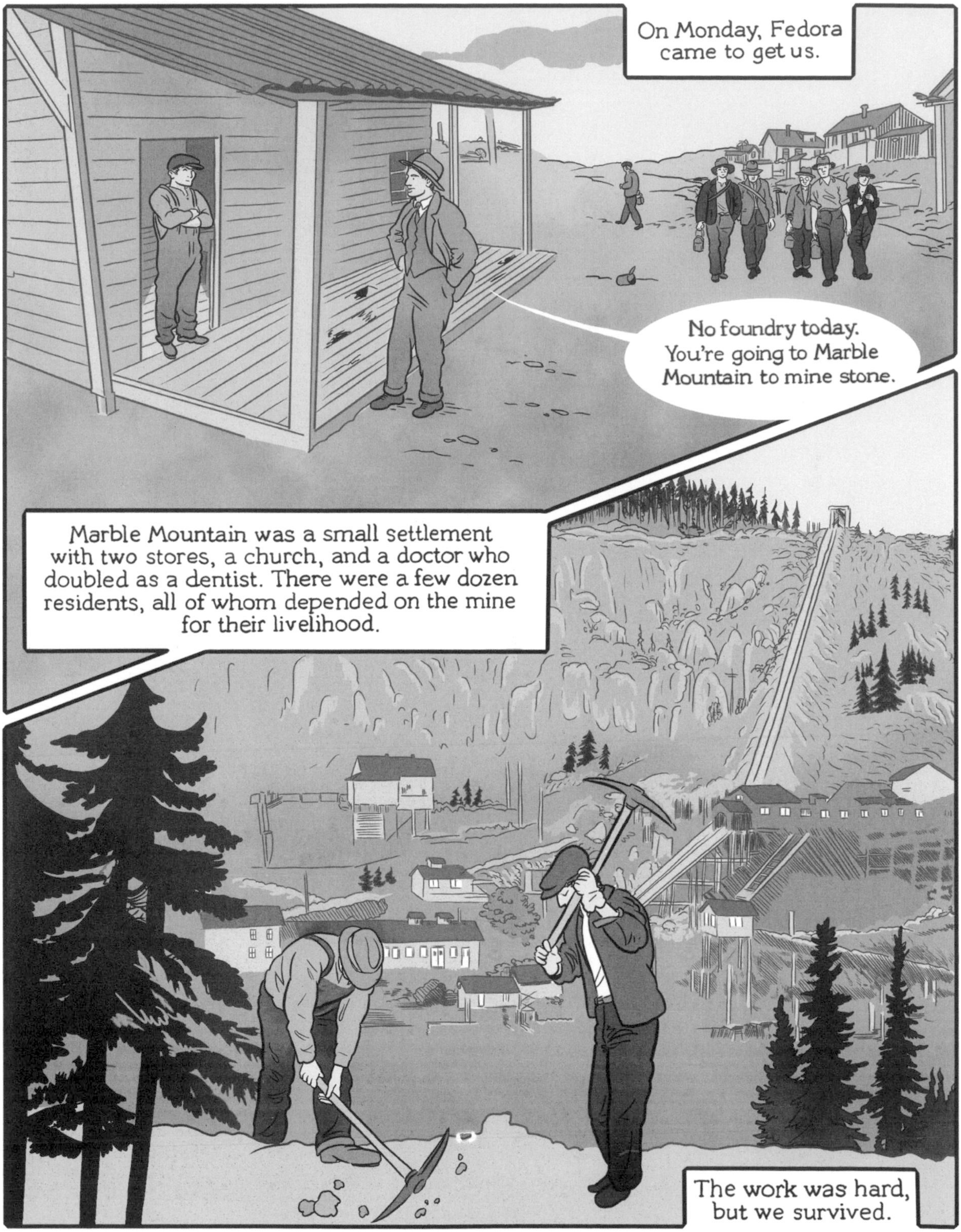
On Monday, Fedora came to get us.
No foundry today. You're going to Marble Mountain to mine stone.
Marble Mountain was a small settlement with two stores, a church, and a doctor who doubled as a dentist. There were a few dozen residents, all of whom depended on the mine for their livelihood.
The work was hard, but we survived.

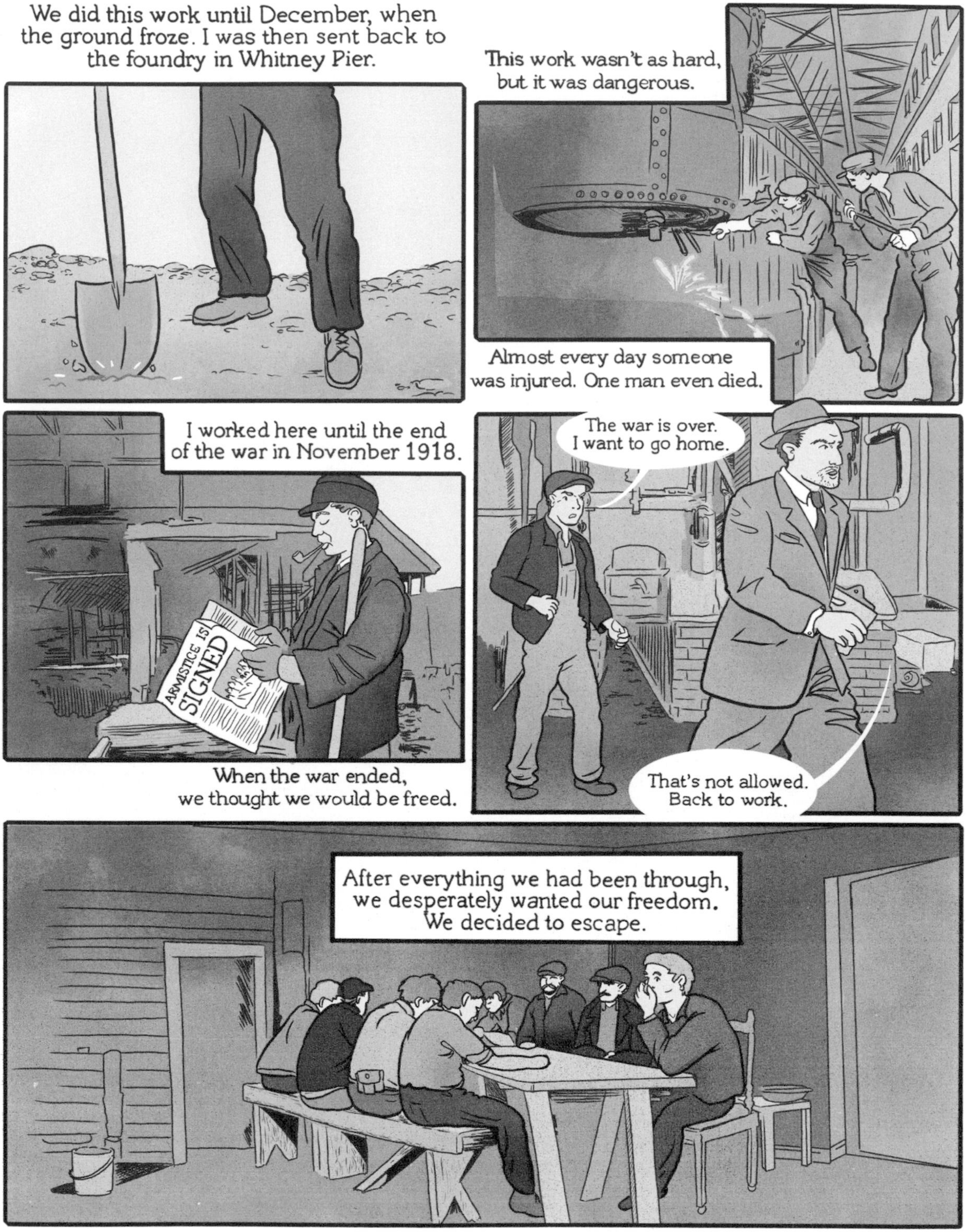
We did this work until December, when the ground froze. I was then sent back to the foundry in Whitney Pier.
This work wasn't as hard, but it was dangerous.
Almost every day someone was injured. One man even died.
I worked here until the end of the war in November 1918.
ARMISTICE IS SIGNED
When the war ended, we thought we would be freed.
The war is over. I want to go home.
That's not allowed. Back to work.
After everything we had been through, we desperately wanted our freedom. We decided to escape.

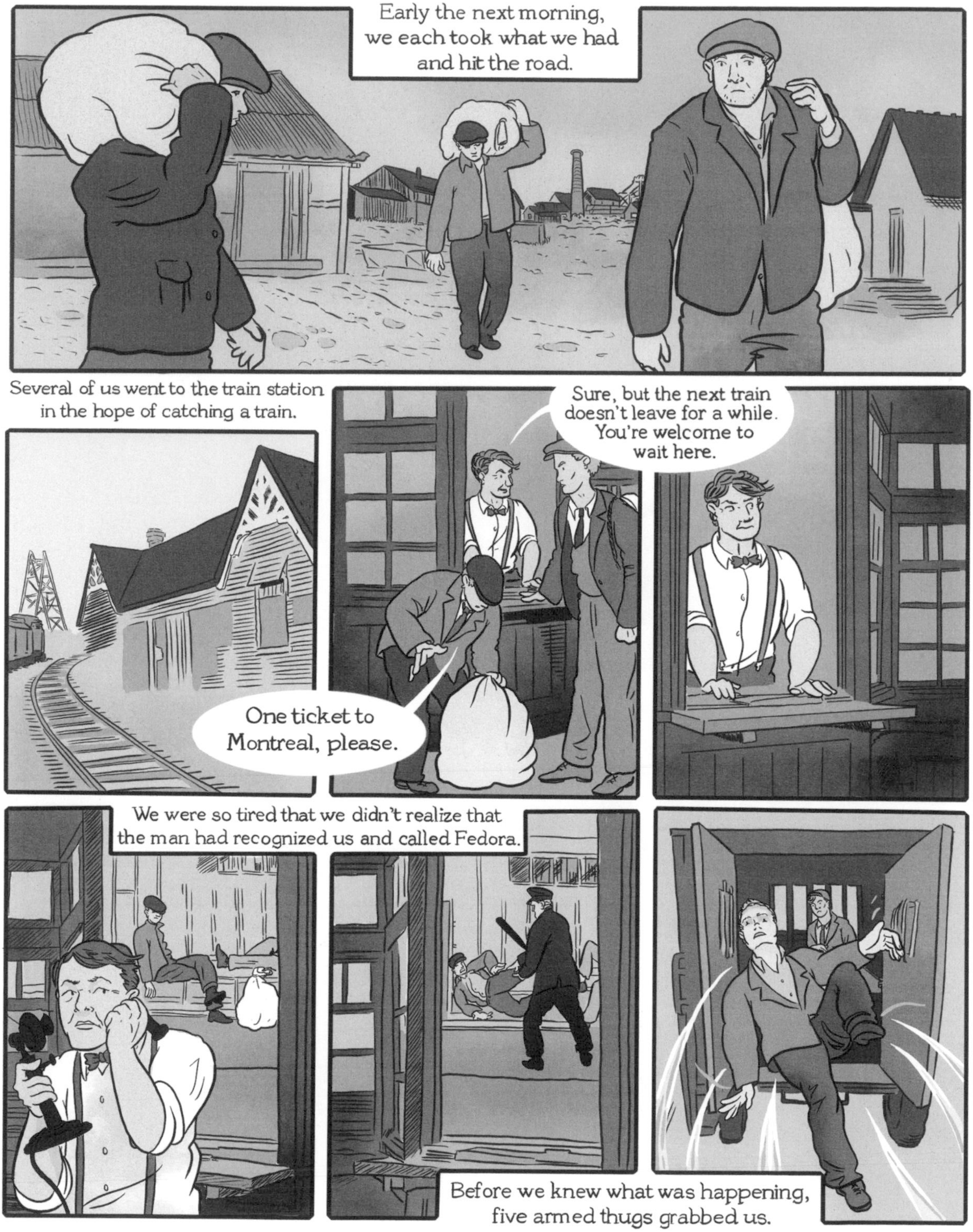
Early the next morning, we each took what we had and hit the road.
Several of us went to the train station in the hope of catching a train.
One ticket to Montreal, please.
Sure, but the next train doesn't leave for a while. You're welcome to wait here.
We were so tired that we didn't realize that the man had recognized us and called Fedora.
Before we knew what was happening, five armed thugs grabbed us.

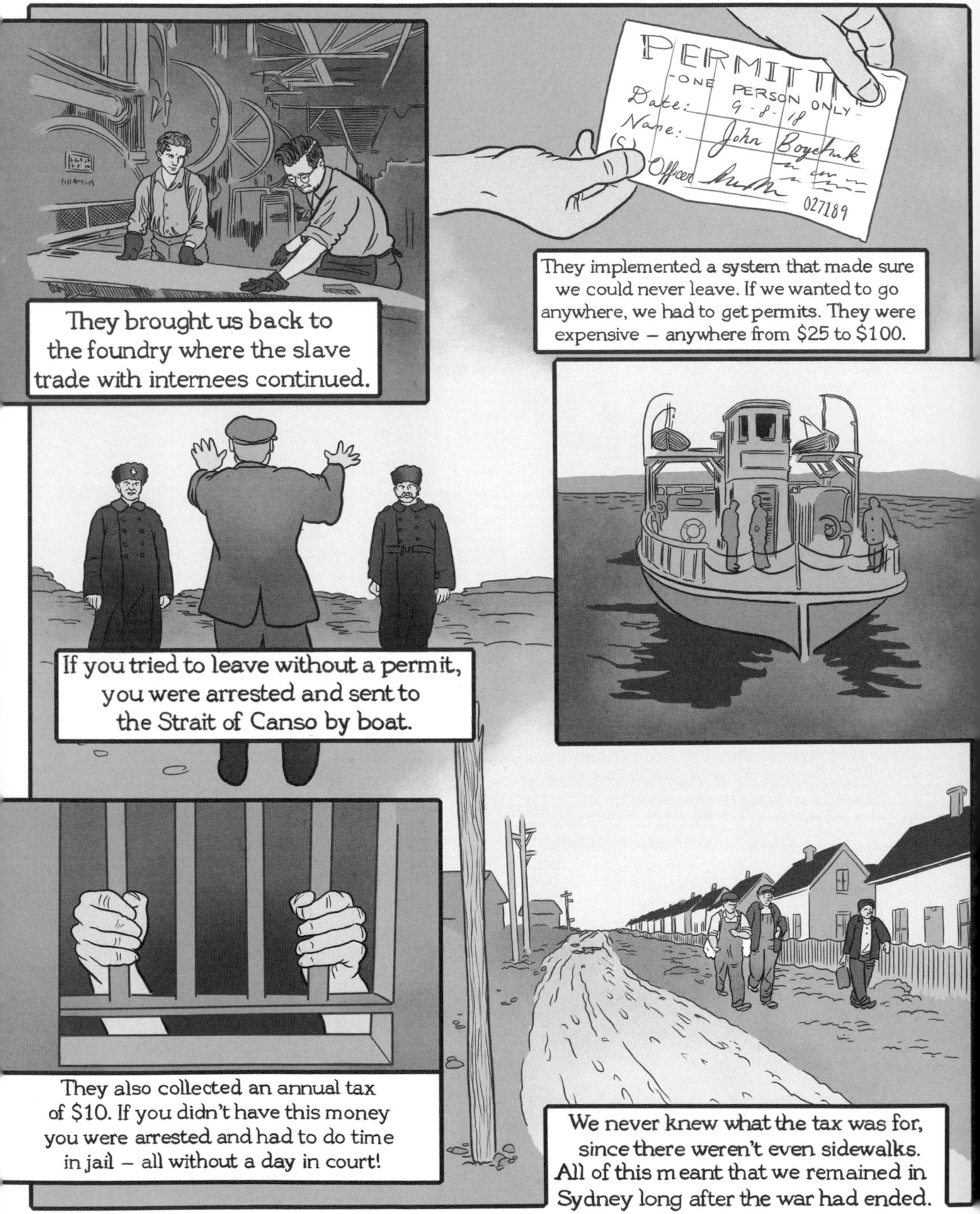
They brought us back to the foundry where the slave trade with internees continued.
PERMIT -ONE PERSON ONLY- Date: 9-8-18 Name: John Boychuk Officer 027189
They implemented a system that made sure we could never leave. If we wanted to go anywhere, we had to get permits. They were expensive – anywhere from $25 to $100.
If you tried to leave without a permit, you were arrested and sent to the Strait of Canso by boat.
They also collected an annual tax of $10. If you didn't have this money you were arrested and had to do time in jail – all without a day in court!
We never knew what the tax was for, since there weren't even sidewalks. All of this meant that we remained in Sydney long after the war had ended.

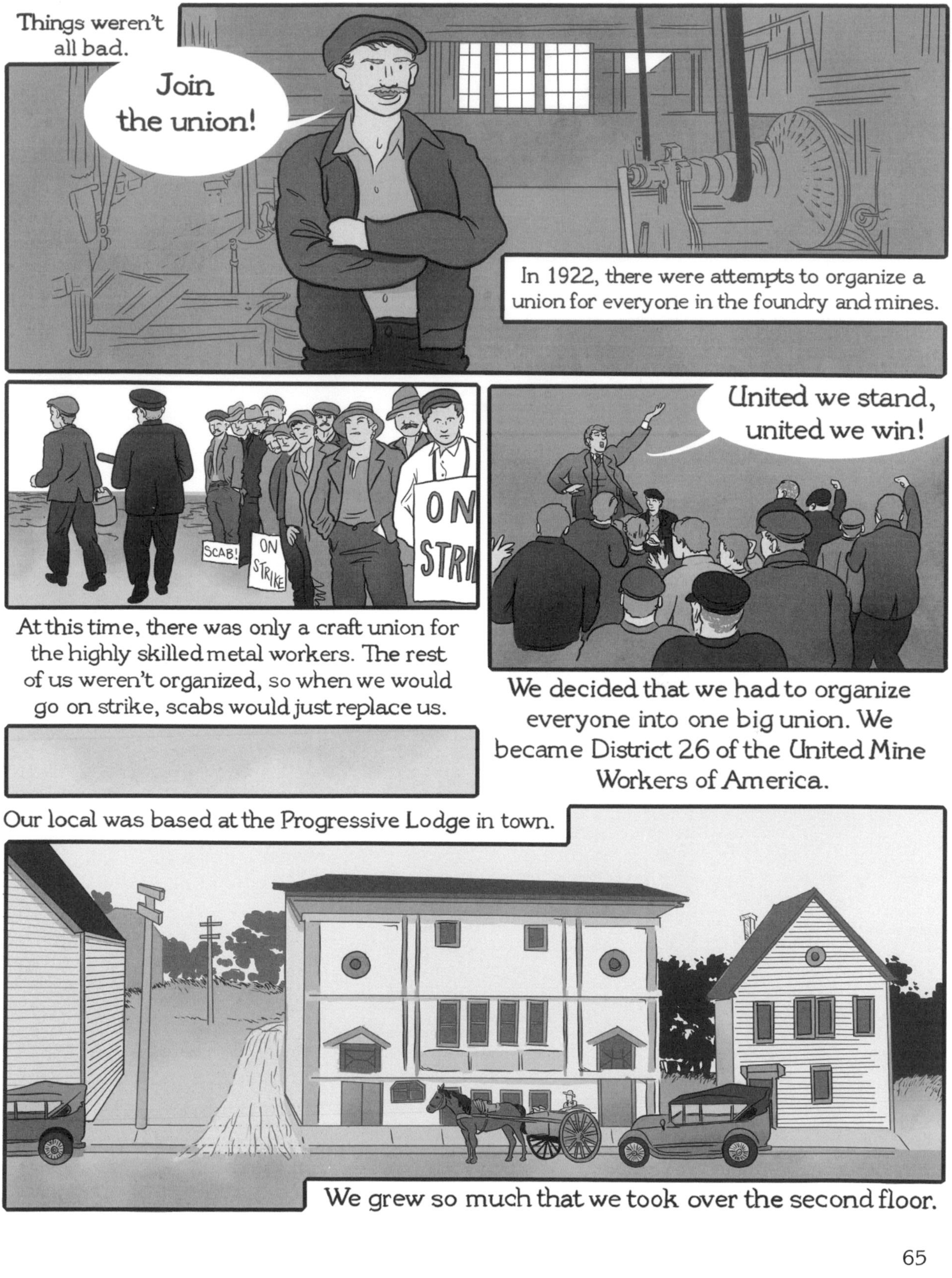

Things weren't all bad.
Join the union!
In 1922, there were attempts to organize a union for everyone in the foundry and mines.
SCAB!
ON STRIKE
ON STRI
At this time, there was only a craft union for the highly skilled metal workers. The rest of us weren't organized, so when we would go on strike, scabs would just replace us.
United we stand, united we win!
We decided that we had to organize everyone into one big union. We became District 26 of the United Mine Workers of America.
Our local was based at the Progressive Lodge in town.
We grew so much that we took over the second floor.

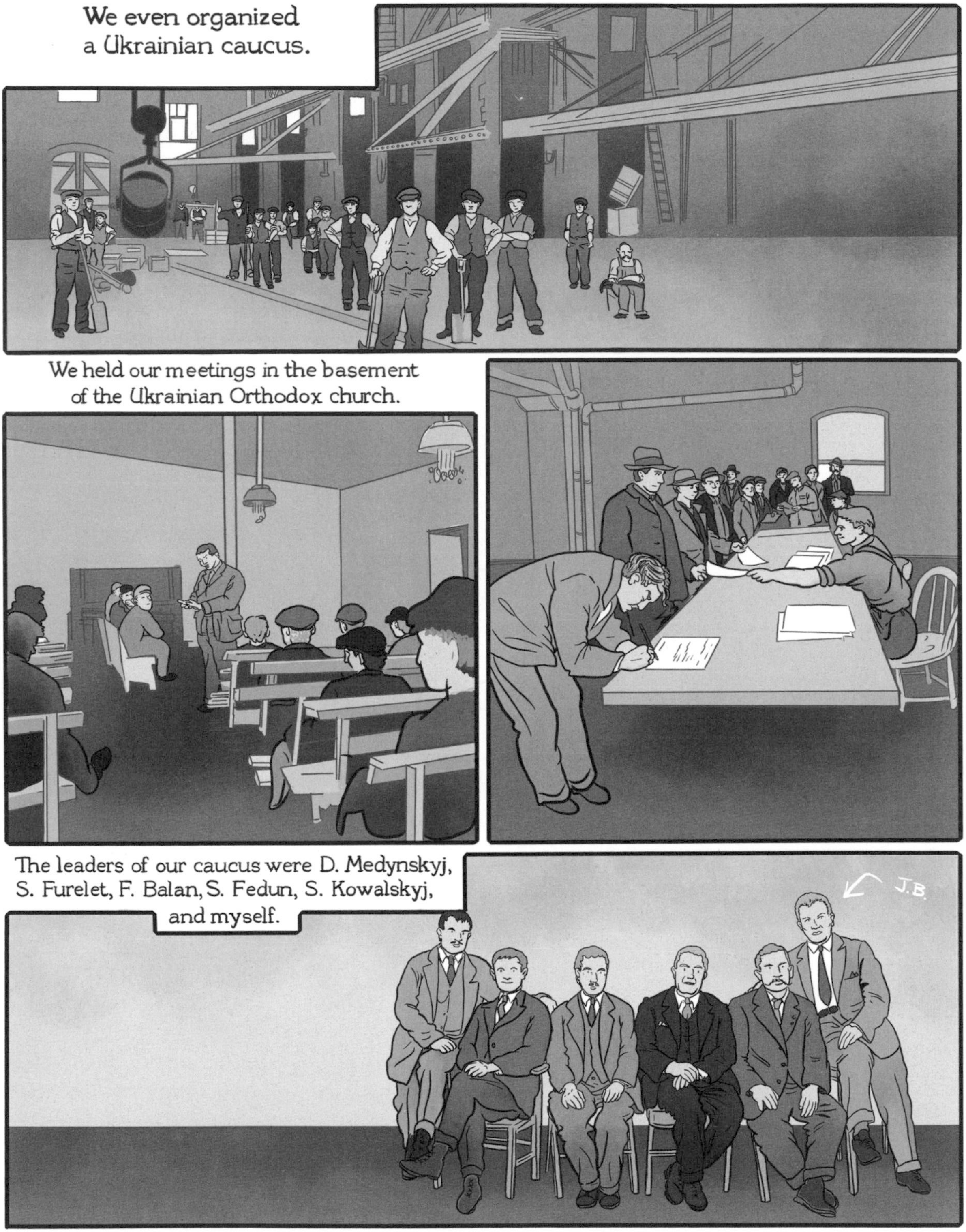
We even organized
a Ukrainian caucus.
We held our meetings in the basement
of the Ukrainian Orthodox church.
The leaders of our caucus were D. Medynskyj,
S. Furelet, F. Balan, S. Fedun, S. Kowalskyj,
and myself.
J.B.

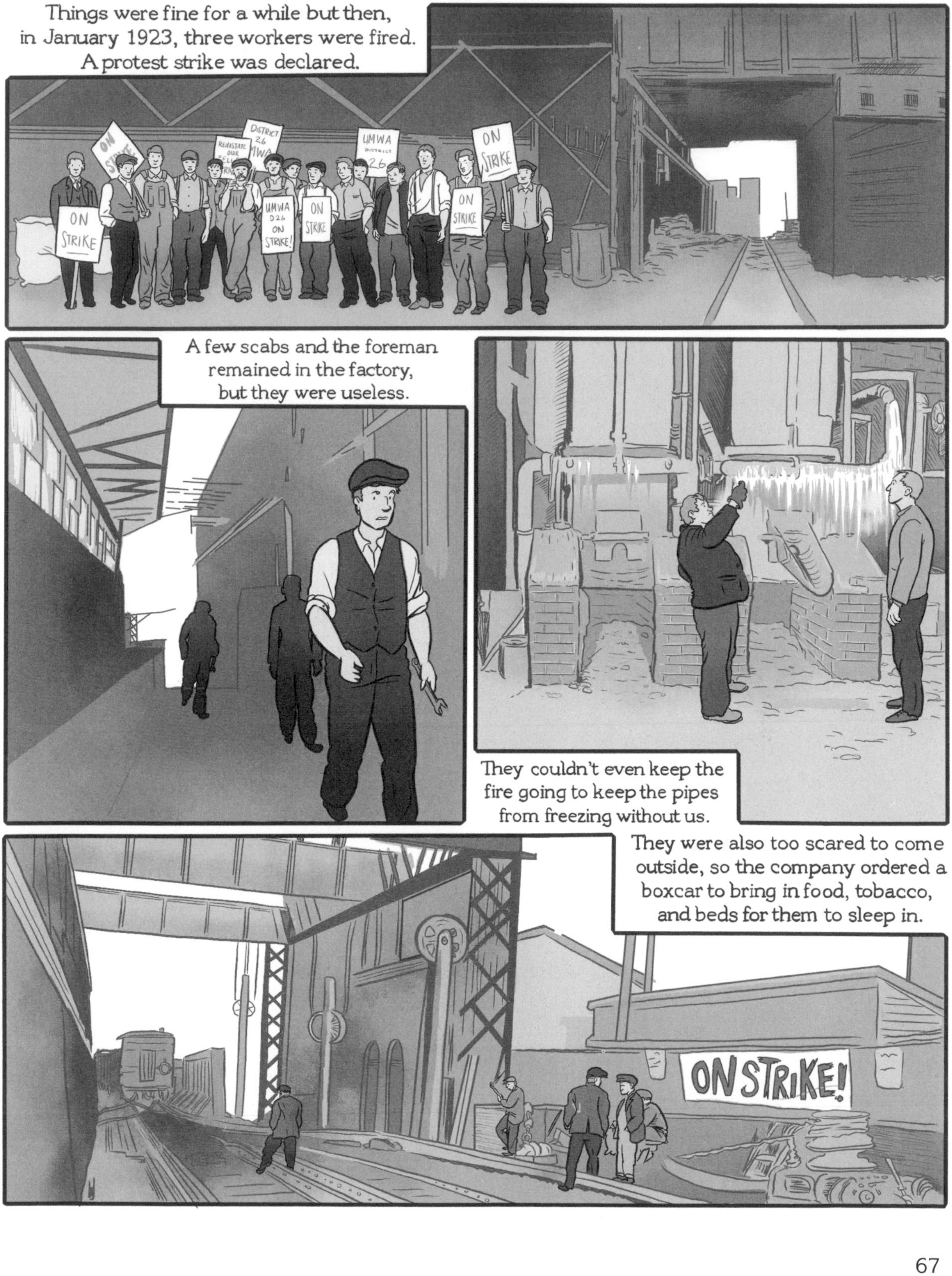
Things were fine for a while but then, in January 1923, three workers were fired. A protest strike was declared.
ON STRIKE
DISTRICT 26 UMWA
UMWA DISTRICT 26
ON STRIKE
UMWA D26 ON STRIKE!
ON STRIKE
ON STRIKE
ON STRIKE
A few scabs and the foreman remained in the factory, but they were useless.
They couldn't even keep the fire going to keep the pipes from freezing without us.
They were also too scared to come outside, so the company ordered a boxcar to bring in food, tobacco, and beds for them to sleep in.
ON STRIKE!

When a boxcar got close to the gate, we'd stop it for inspection.

One time it wasn't just food and beds in there...

Fedora!

To make sure he didn't come back, we escorted him home.

He was yelled at the whole way.

Scab!

Traitor!

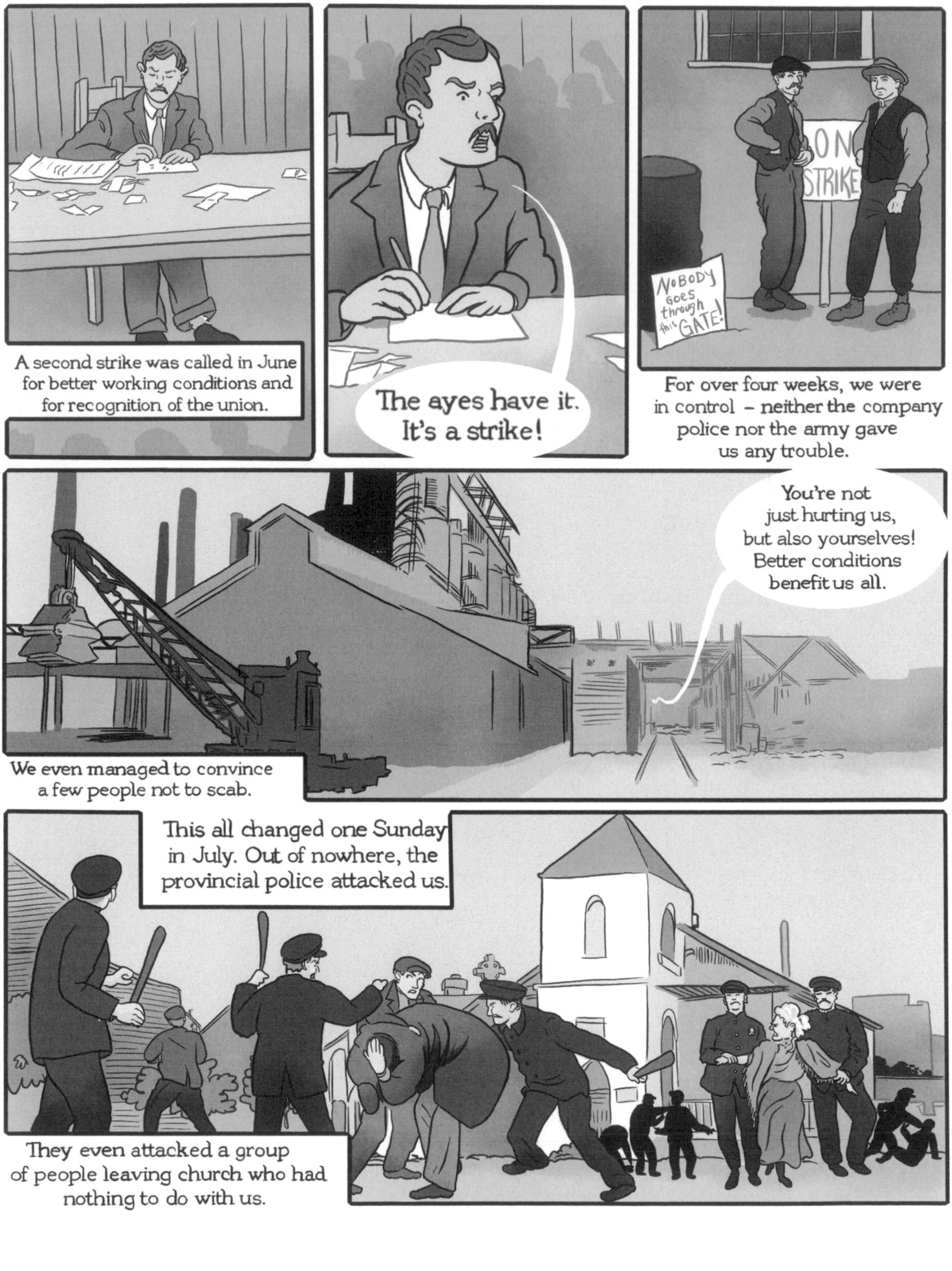
A second strike was called in June for better working conditions and for recognition of the union.
The ayes have it. It's a strike!
ON STRIKE
NOBODY GOES through this GATE!
For over four weeks, we were in control – neither the company police nor the army gave us any trouble.
You're not just hurting us, but also yourselves! Better conditions benefit us all.
We even managed to convince a few people not to scab.
This all changed one Sunday in July. Out of nowhere, the provincial police attacked us.
They even attacked a group of people leaving church who had nothing to do with us.

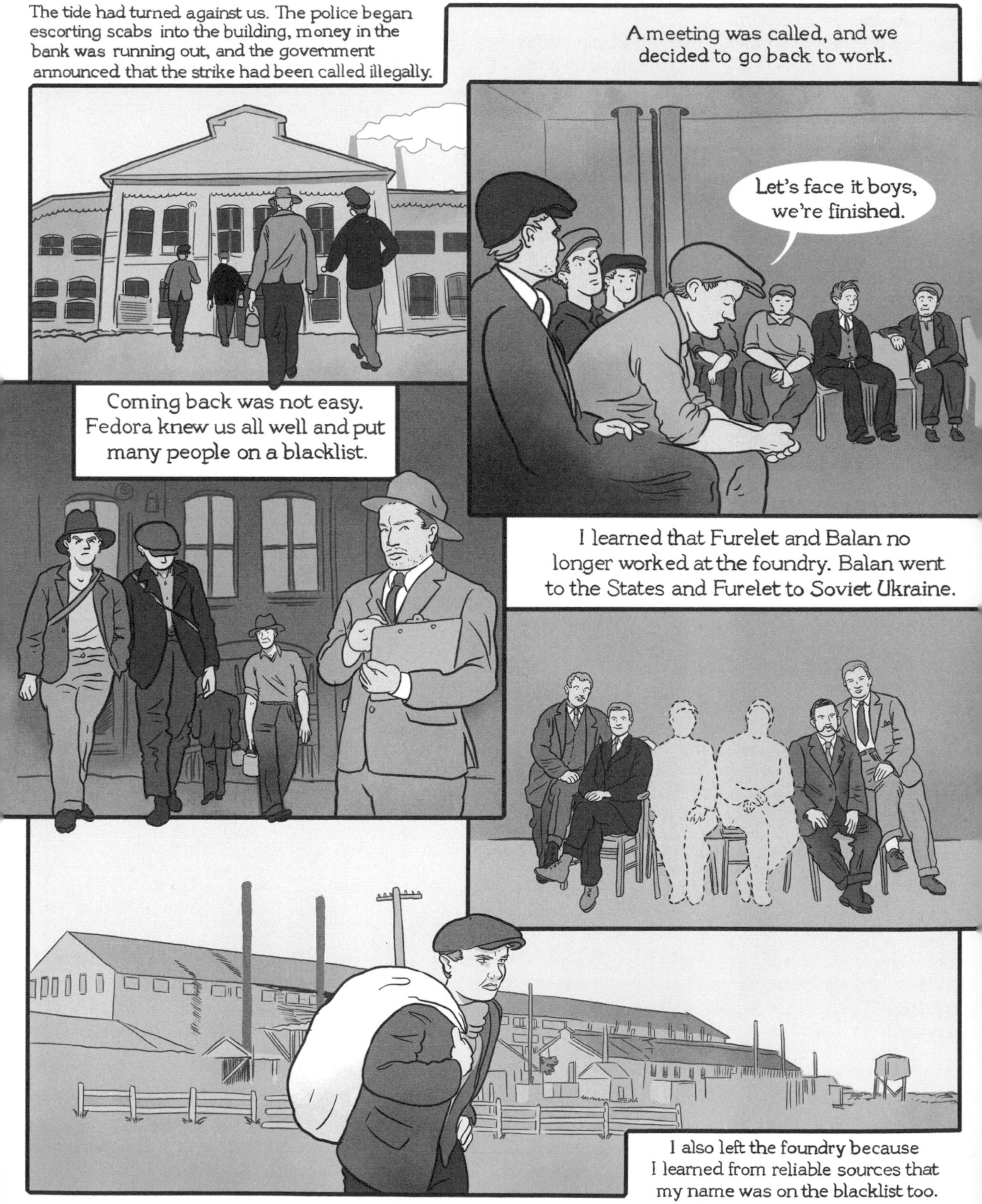

The tide had turned against us. The police began escorting scabs into the building, money in the bank was running out, and the government announced that the strike had been called illegally.
A meeting was called, and we decided to go back to work.
Let's face it boys, we're finished.
Coming back was not easy. Fedora knew us all well and put many people on a blacklist.
I learned that Furelet and Balan no longer worked at the foundry. Balan went to the States and Furelet to Soviet Ukraine.
I also left the foundry because I learned from reliable sources that my name was on the blacklist too.

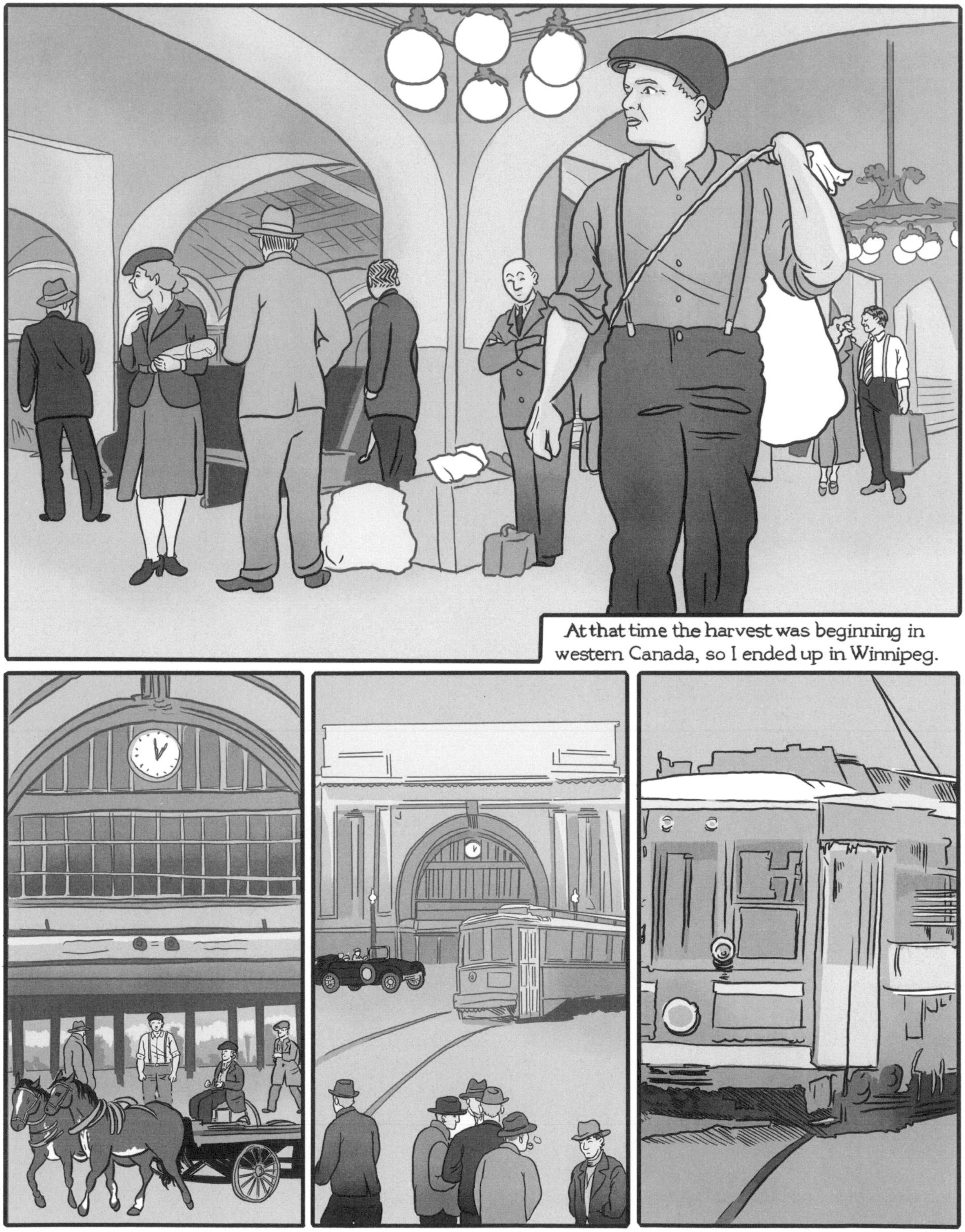
At that time the harvest was beginning in western Canada, so I ended up in Winnipeg.

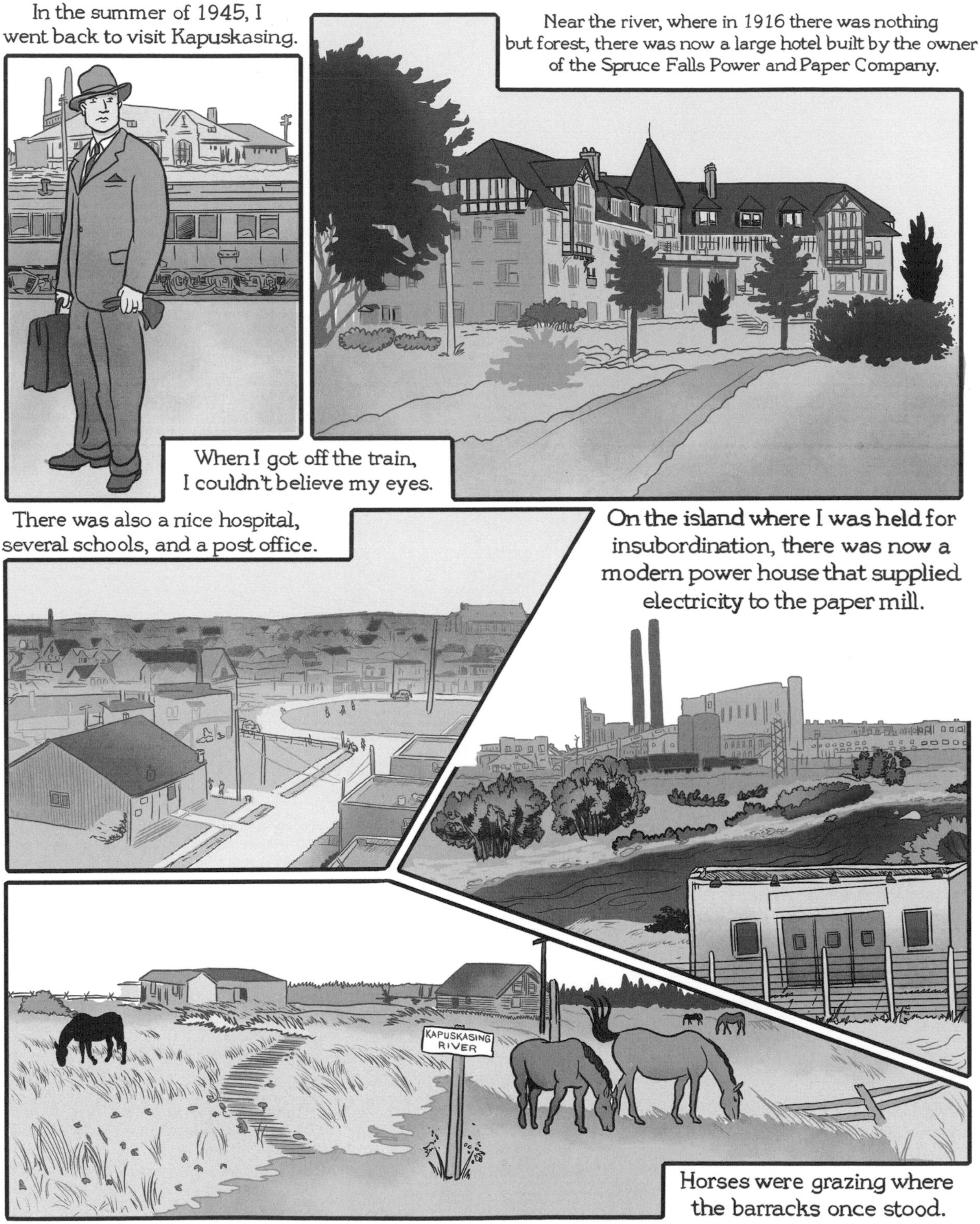
In the summer of 1945, I went back to visit Kapuskasing.
When I got off the train, I couldn't believe my eyes.
Near the river, where in 1916 there was nothing but forest, there was now a large hotel built by the owner of the Spruce Falls Power and Paper Company.
There was also a nice hospital, several schools, and a post office.
On the island where I was held for insubordination, there was now a modern power house that supplied electricity to the paper mill.
KAPUSKASING RIVER
Horses were grazing where the barracks once stood.

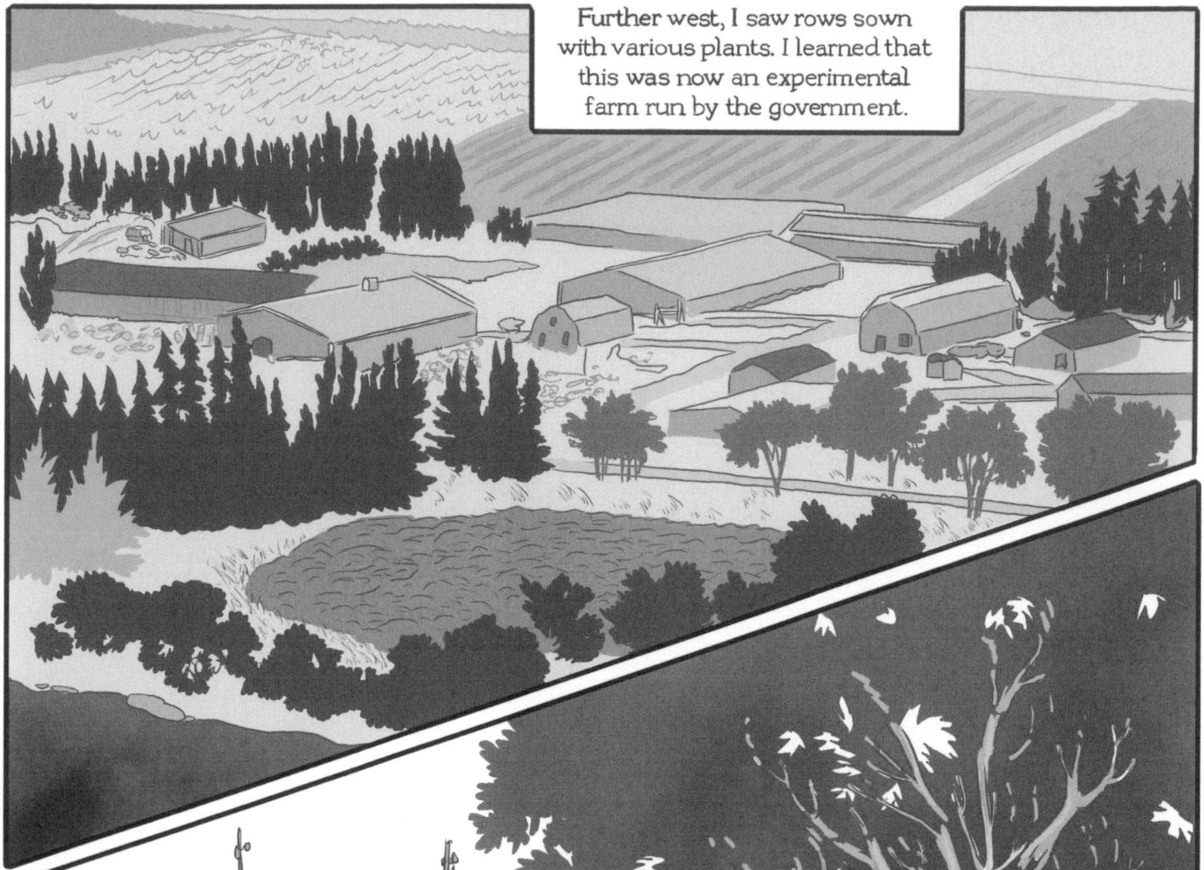
Further west, I saw rows sown with various plants. I learned that this was now an experimental farm run by the government.

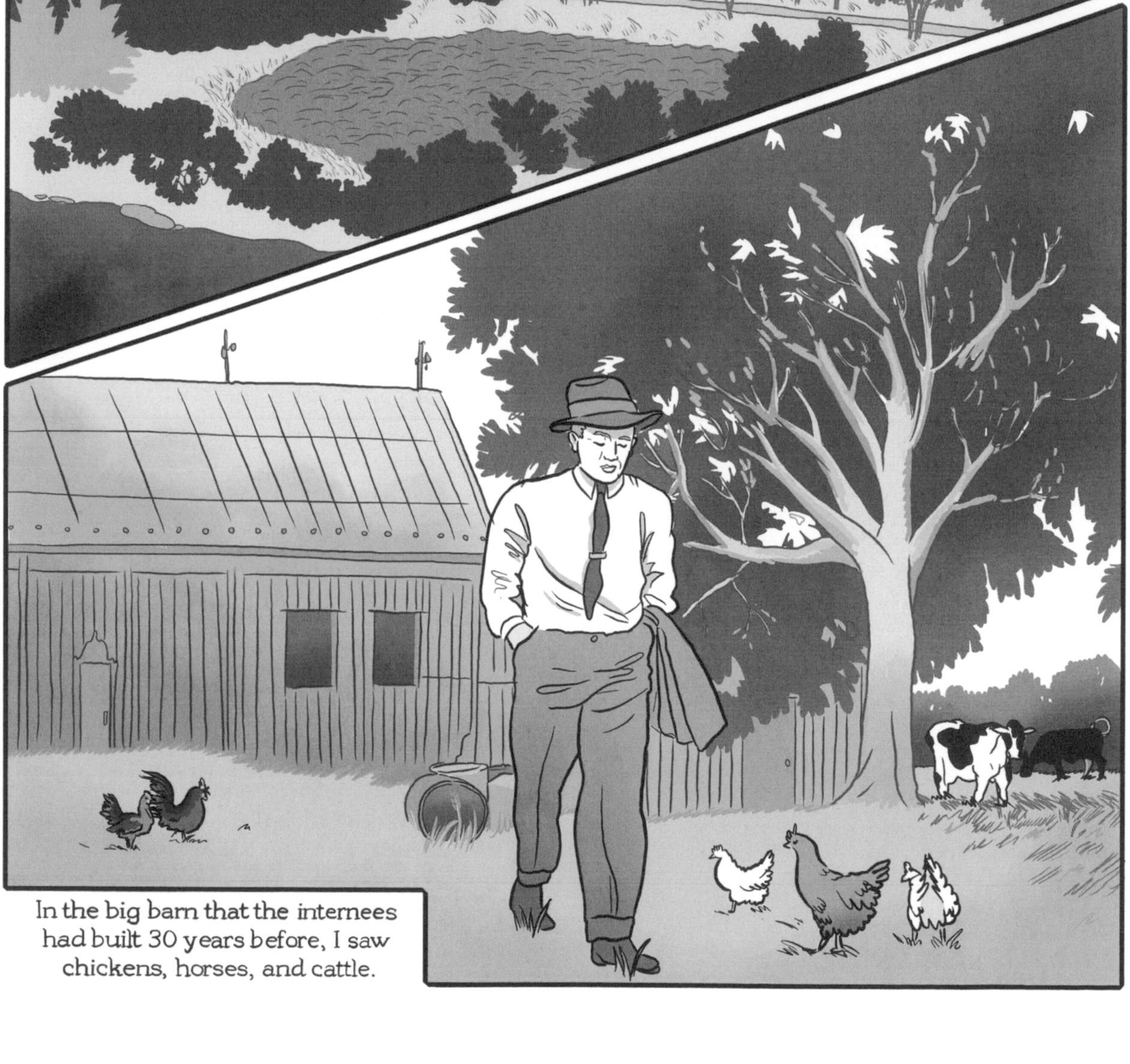
In the big barn that the internees had built 30 years before, I saw chickens, horses, and cattle.

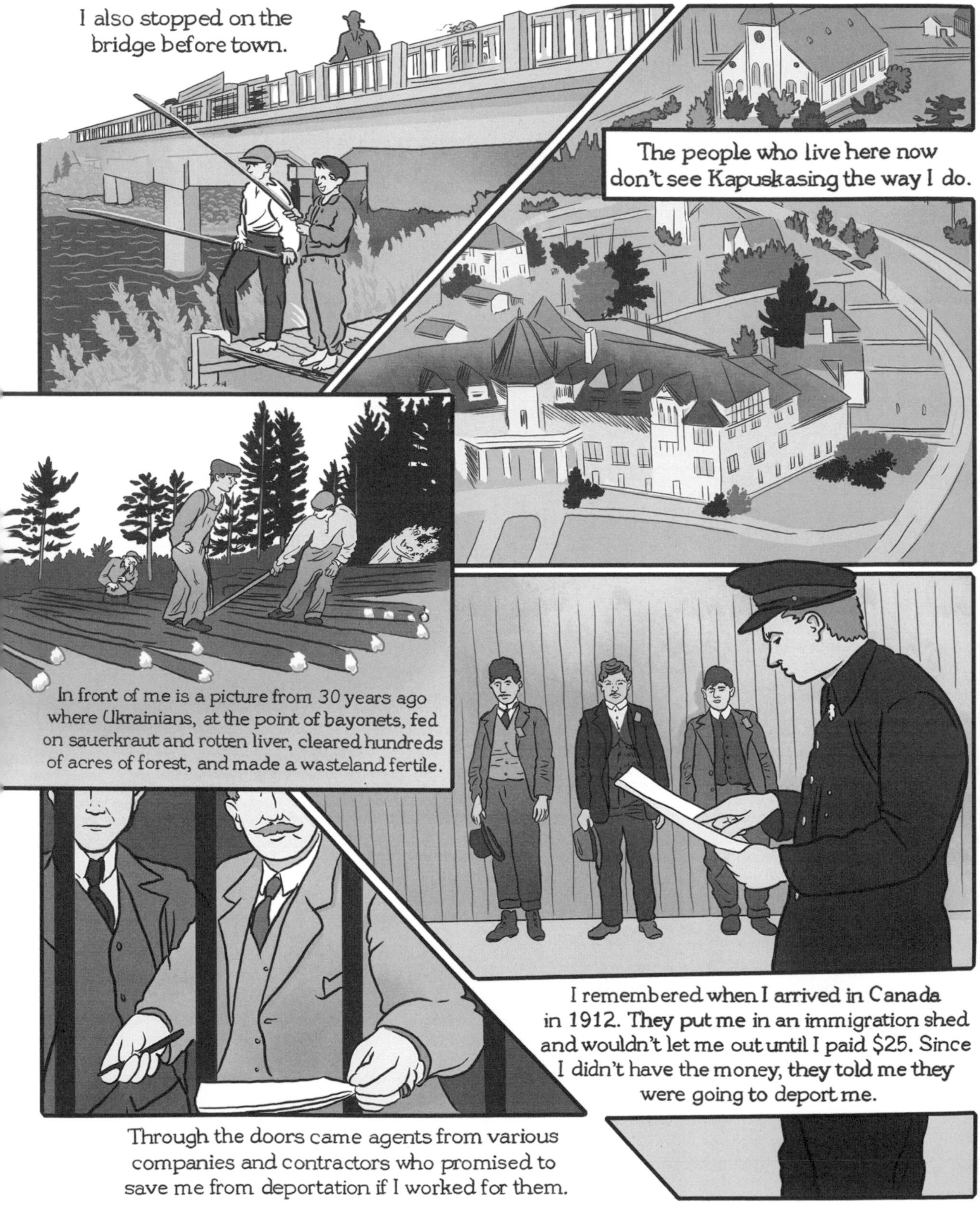
I also stopped on the bridge before town.
The people who live here now don't see Kapuskasing the way I do.
In front of me is a picture from 30 years ago where Ukrainians, at the point of bayonets, fed on sauerkraut and rotten liver, cleared hundreds of acres of forest, and made a wasteland fertile.
I remembered when I arrived in Canada in 1912. They put me in an immigration shed and wouldn't let me out until I paid $25. Since I didn't have the money, they told me they were going to deport me.
Through the doors came agents from various companies and contractors who promised to save me from deportation if I worked for them.

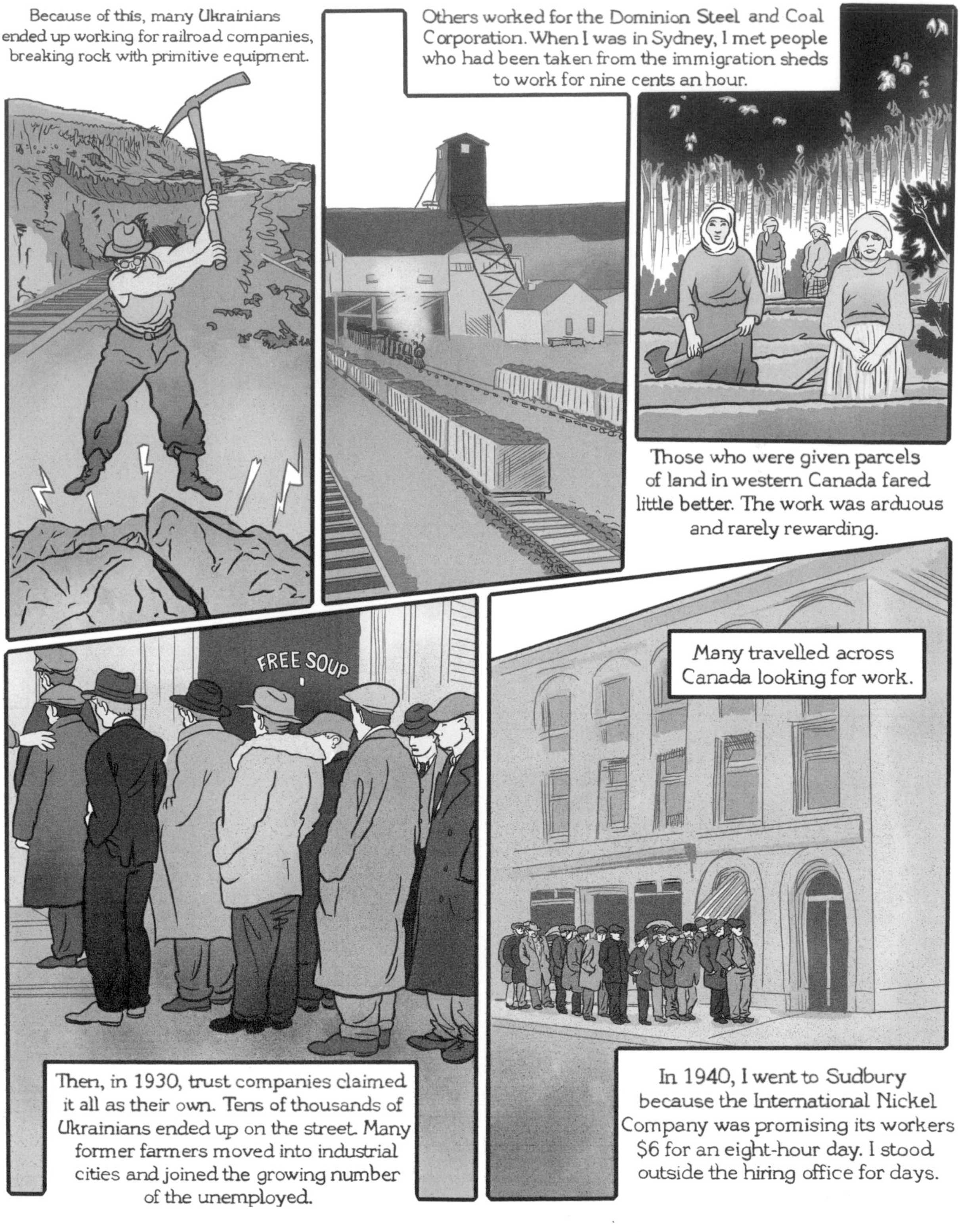
Because of this, many Ukrainians ended up working for railroad companies, breaking rock with primitive equipment.
Others worked for the Dominion Steel and Coal Corporation. When I was in Sydney, I met people who had been taken from the immigration sheds to work for nine cents an hour.
Those who were given parcels of land in western Canada fared little better. The work was arduous and rarely rewarding.
FREE SOUP
Then, in 1930, trust companies claimed it all as their own. Tens of thousands of Ukrainians ended up on the street. Many former farmers moved into industrial cities and joined the growing number of the unemployed.
Many travelled across Canada looking for work.
In 1940, I went to Sudbury because the International Nickel Company was promising its workers $6 for an eight-hour day. I stood outside the hiring office for days.

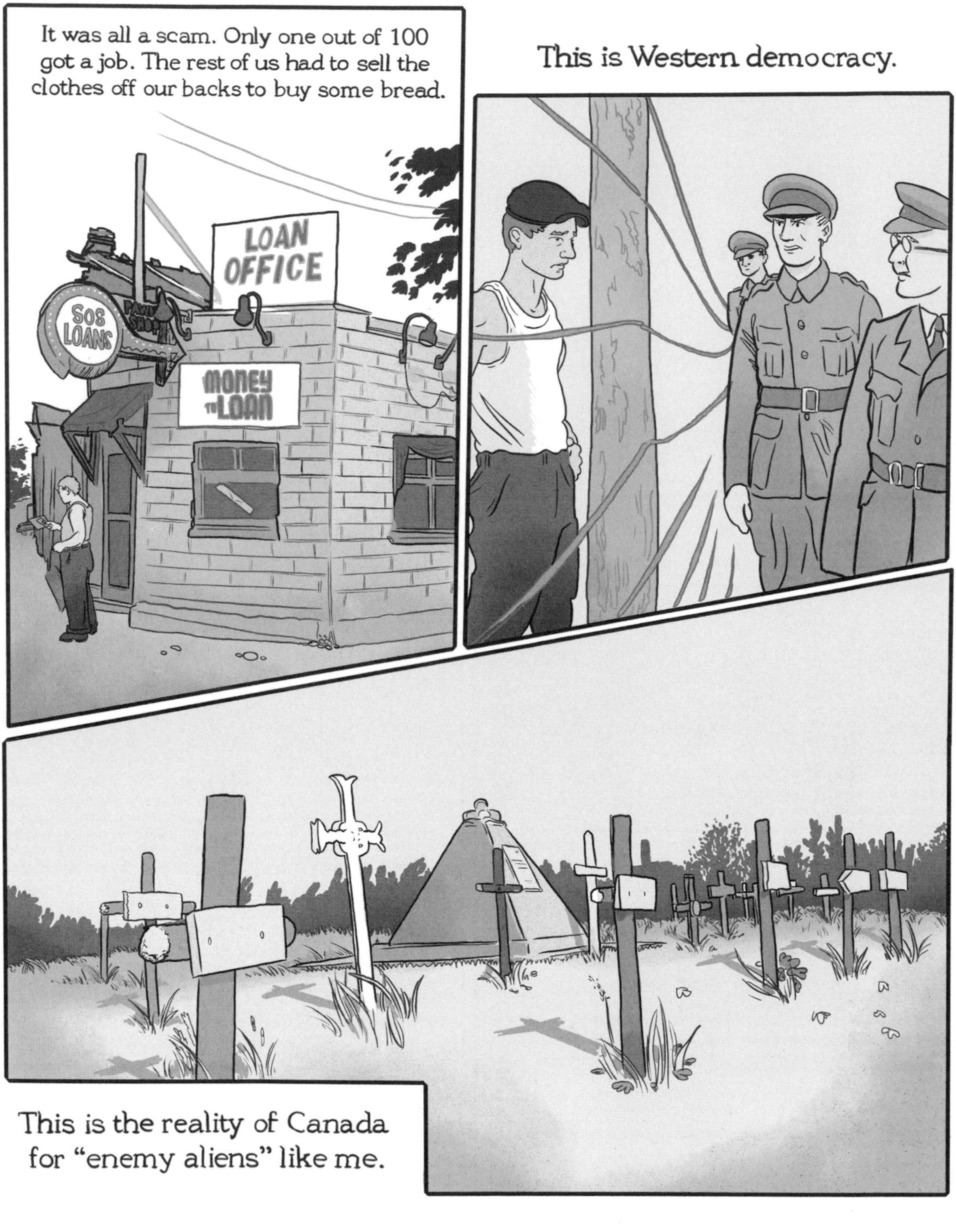
It was all a scam. Only one out of 100 got a job. The rest of us had to sell the clothes off our backs to buy some bread.
LOAN OFFICE
SOS LOANS
PAWN SHOP
MONEY TO LOAN
This is Western democracy.
This is the reality of Canada for "enemy aliens" like me.

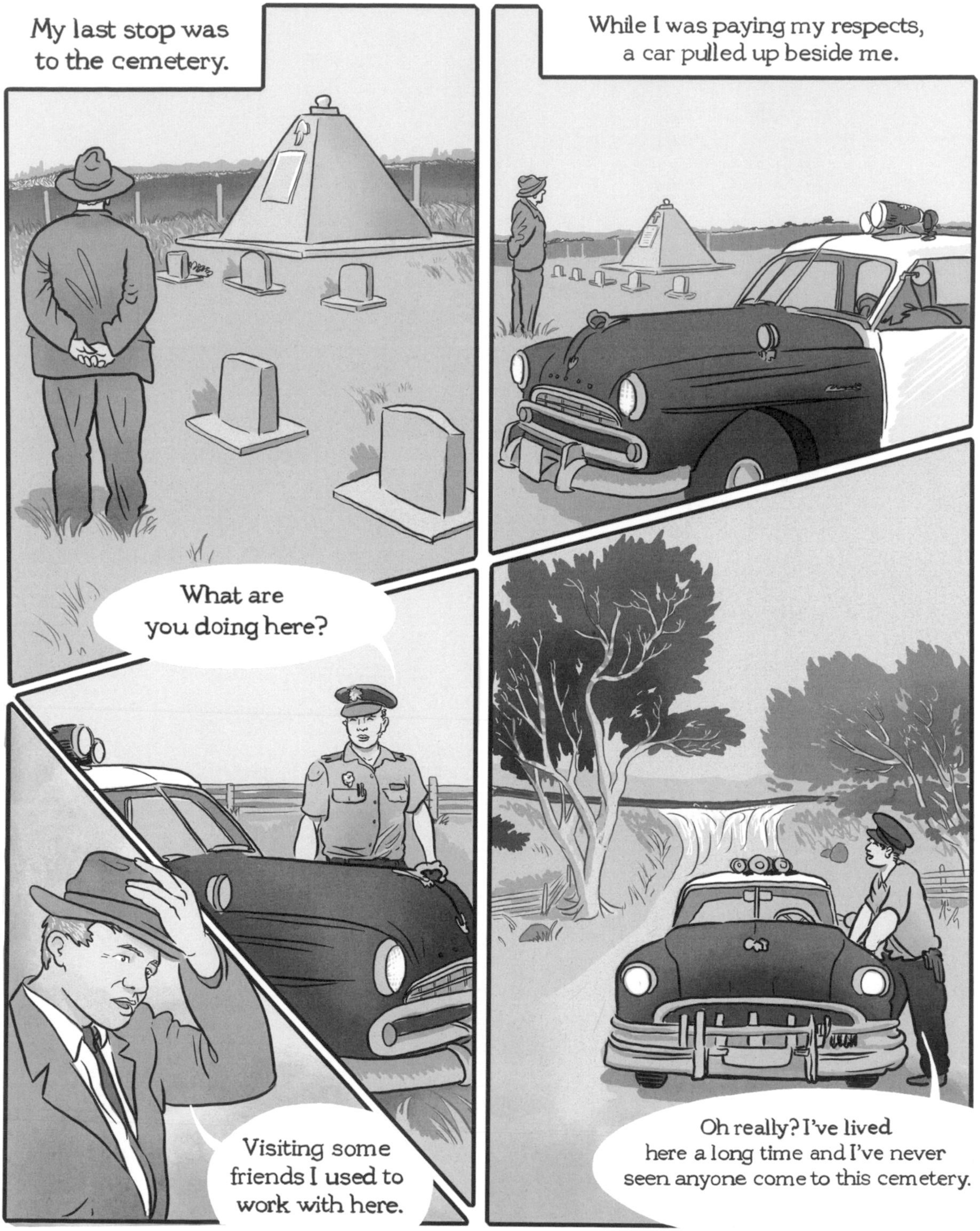
My last stop was to the cemetery.
While I was paying my respects, a car pulled up beside me.
What are you doing here?
Visiting some friends I used to work with here.
Oh really? I've lived here a long time and I've never seen anyone come to this cemetery.

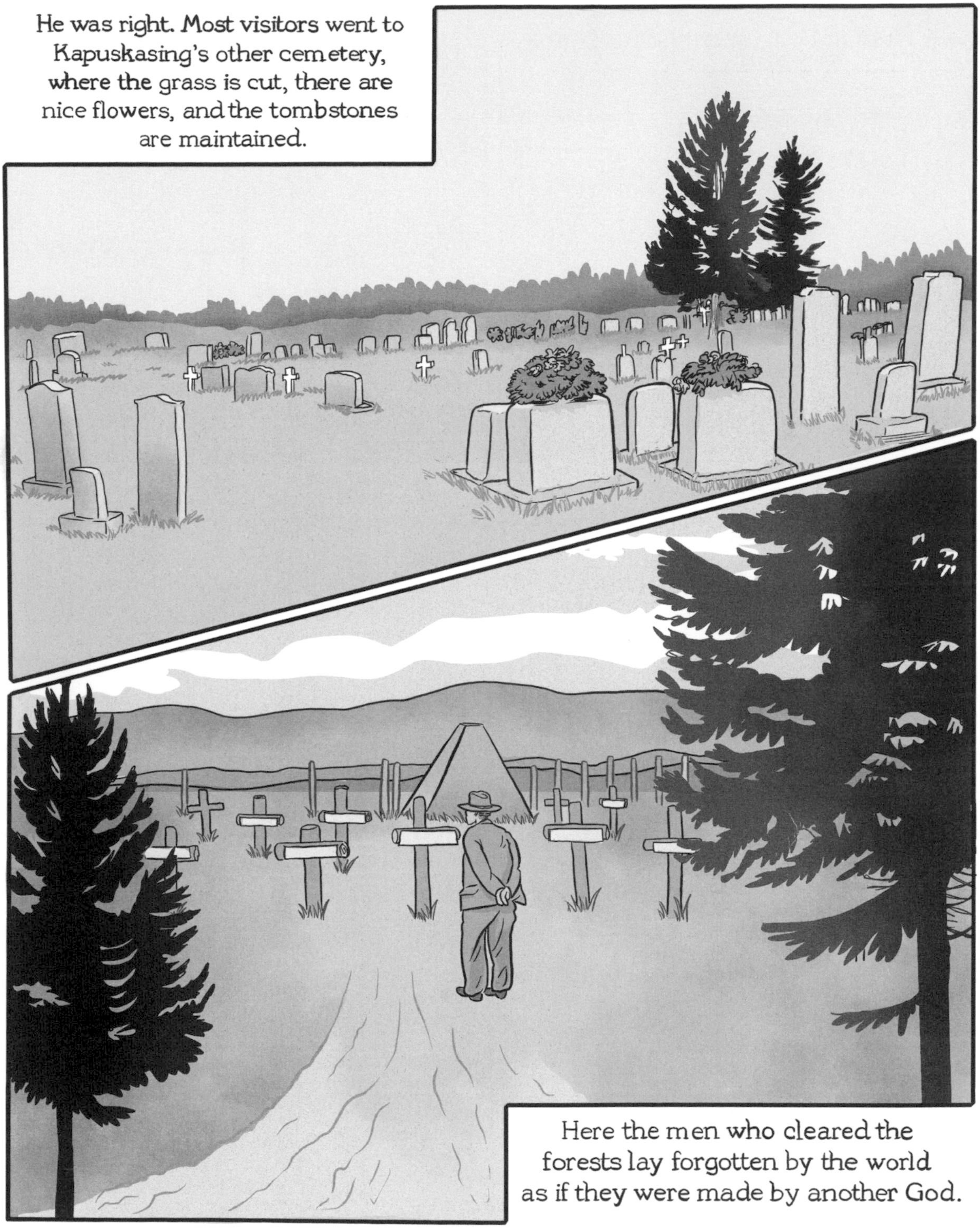
He was right. Most visitors went to Kapuskasing's other cemetery, where the grass is cut, there are nice flowers, and the tombstones are maintained.
Here the men who cleared the forests lay forgotten by the world as if they were made by another God.

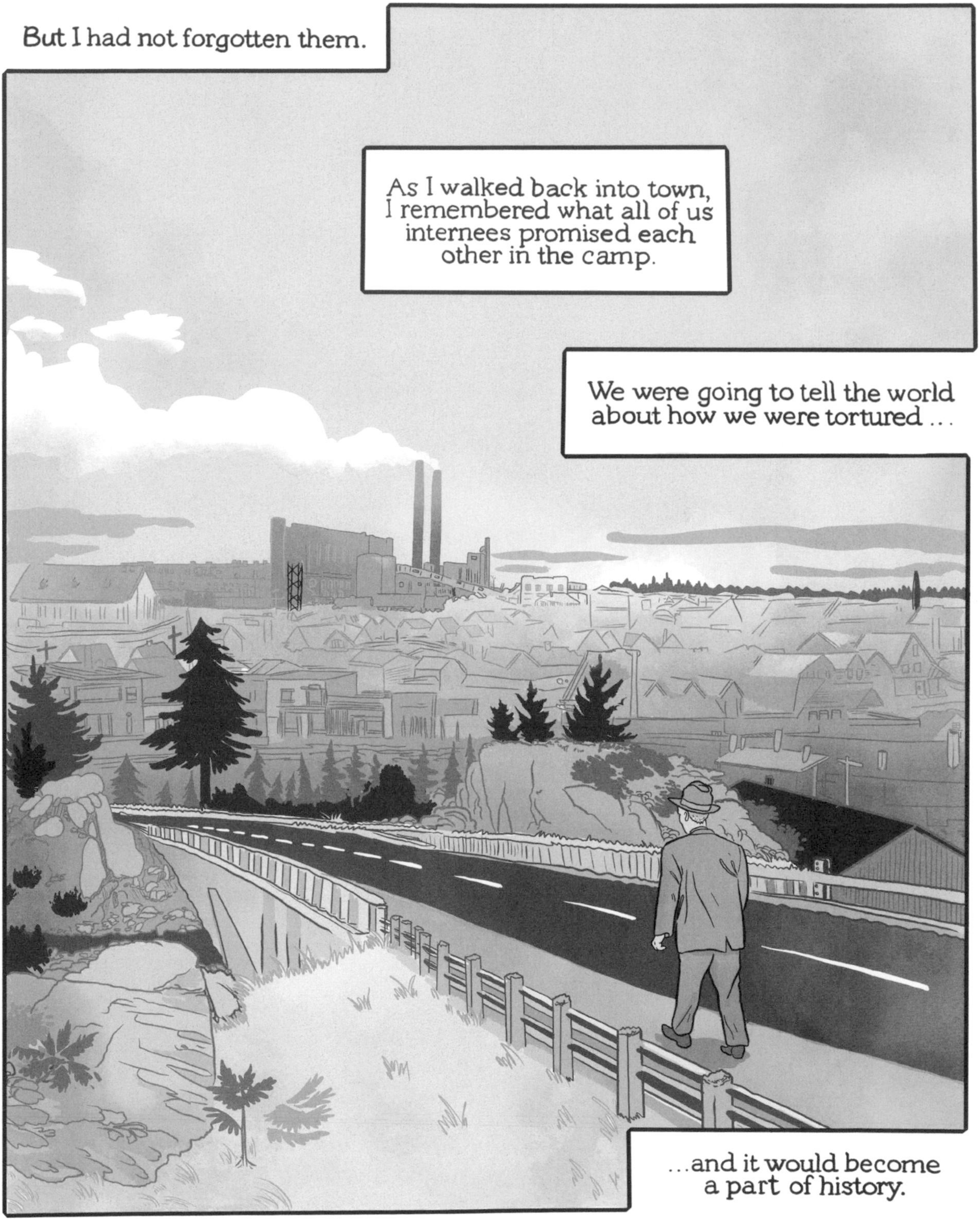
But I had not forgotten them.
As I walked back into town, I remembered what all of us internees promised each other in the camp.
We were going to tell the world about how we were tortured . . .
. . . and it would become a part of history.

Acknowledgements

I would like to thank nicole marie burton, Larissa Stavroff, Mikhail Bjorge, Alexandra Chyczij, Olena Chyczij, Lubomyr Luciuk, Nadia Luciuk, Tilman Lewis, Amanda Crocker, Hugh Goldring, Rhonda Hinther, Ernest Gyidel, Paulina Sawarna, and Ugurhan Berkok.

—*Kassandra Luciuk*

The art in the pages of *Enemy Alien* came to be with the assistance of many. I would like to thank Kassandra Luciuk, JQ Hannah, Penny Goldsmith, Hugh Goldring, Nancy Davis Halifax, Philip & Marianne, Sean & Dmitri, Kara Sievewright, Amanda Crocker, and Devin Clancy. Your contribution, big or small, is greatly appreciated.

—*nicole marie burton*

Sources

First-person memoir: From the privately held Stavroff-Krawchuk
    collection.
Poem, page 16: Taras Shevchenko, "Calamity Again," *Selections*, trans.
    John Weir (Toronto: The Ukrainian Canadian, 1961).

Further Reading

Donald Avery, *Dangerous Foreigners: European Immigrant Workers and
    Labour Radicalism in Canada, 1896–1932* (Toronto: McClelland
    and Stewart, 1979).
David Carter, *Behind Canadian Barbed Wire: Alien, Refugee,
    and Prisoner of War Camps in Canada, 1914–1946* (Calgary:
    Tumbleweed Press, 1980).
James Farney and Bohdan Kordan, "The Predicament of Belonging:
    The Status of Enemy Aliens in Canada, 1914," *Journal of Canadian
    Studies* 39,1 (Winter 2005), 74–89.
Rhonda Hinther and Jim Mochoruk, eds., *Civilian Internment in
    Canada: Histories and Legacies* (Winnipeg: University of Manitoba
    Press, 2020).
Franca Iacovetta, Roberto Perin, and Angelo Principe, eds., *Enemies
    Within: Italian and Other Internees in Canada and Abroad* (Toronto:
    University of Toronto Press, 2000).
Bohdan Kordan, *No Free Man: Canada, the Great War, and the
    Enemy Alien Experience* (Montreal and Kingston: McGill-Queen's
    University Press, 2016).
Bohdan Kordan and Peter Melnycky, *In the Shadow of the Rockies: Diary
    of the Castle Mountain Internment Camp, 1915–1917* (Edmonton:
    University of Alberta Press, 1991).
Lubomyr Luciuk, *In Fear of the Barbed Wire Fence: Canada's First
    National Internment Operations and the Ukrainian Canadians,
    1914–1920* (Kingston: Kashtan Press, 2001).
Lubomyr Luciuk, *Without Just Cause: Canada's First National
    Internment Operations and the Ukrainian Canadians* (Kingston:
    Kashtan Press, 2006).
Myron Momryk, "The Royal Canadian Mounted Police and the
    Surveillance of the Ukrainian Community in Canada," *Journal of
    Ukrainian Studies* 28,2 (Winter 2003), 89–112.

Frances Swyripa and John Herd Thompson, eds., *Loyalties in Conflict: Ukrainians in Canada during the Great War* (Edmonton: Canadian Institute of Ukrainian Studies, 1983).

Bill Waiser, *Park Prisoners: The Untold Story of Western Canada's National Parks, 1915–1946* (Saskatoon: Fifth House Publishers, 1995).

Kassandra Luciuk is a historian interested in the Ukrainian experience in Canada.

nicole marie burton is a comic artist and children's book illustrator living in Ontario. Her published works include *The Boy Who Walked Backwards*, *The Beast: Making a Living on a Dying Planet*, and "Coal Mountain," part of the comics anthology *Drawn to Change: Graphic Histories of Working-Class Struggle*. She is a founding member of the Ad Astra Comix publishing collective.